Mental Health and the Christian

By

Glory Elofuke

Copyright @ Dr. Glory Elofuke 2021

The right of the author has been asserted by her in accordance with the copyright writing, designs and patent act of the United Kingdom.

A catalogue copy of this book is available in the British Library.

All rights reserved. No part of this book may be reproduced, stored or transmitted by any means whether auditory, graphic, mechanical, or electronic without the written permission of the author, except in the case of brief excerpts used in critical articles and reviews. Unauthorized reproduction of any part of this work is illegal and punishable by law.

Unless otherwise noted, the author and the publisher make no explicit guarantees as the accuracy of the information contained in this book may differ based on individual experiences and context.

For enquiries, email: info@gelofuke@gmail.com

Dedication

This book is dedicated to you (the reader) and the many people living with mental illness. It is my sincere hope that you find answers to burning questions and signposts to help you. I also hope that you get to realize that you are not alone.

Acknowledgement

The completion of this book could not have been possible without the support of many who encouraged me along the way. Your kind words of support are deeply appreciated and gratefully acknowledged.

I owe a debt of Gratitude to Pastor (Dr.) Chris Gbenle and Pastor Mrs. Nike Gbenle, for their unrelenting spiritual support, especially to Pastor Chris for a painstaking review of the original manuscript and for writing the Foreword as well, thank you very much sir.

Many thanks to my colleague and brother, Dr. Kunle Adeyemi for also reviewing the original manuscript and much more.

Deep appreciation to Pastor Stanley Okosodo, Dr. Zak Hani, Dr. Otefe Otebi, Dr. Adaeze Ifezulike and Dr. Julius Essem, for sharing their perspectives on mental health issues through link videos, leading up to the publication of this book.

Special thanks to my best friend and book coach, Florence Igboayaka for her support and for providing the platform that made this dream a reality.

To my long-suffering husband and gifted sons, who stepped up and allowed me the sterile cockpit to focus on my writing, your support is more than words can express. Thank you.

Above all, to the Almighty God, my inspiration, the author of knowledge and wisdom, for His reckless love and good graces.

TABLE OF CONTENT

Dedication 3

Acknowledgement 4

Foreword 9

INTRODUCTION 12

CHAPTER 1: A DEEP DIVE 18

   Why Mental Health? 18
   HOW THE MIND WORKS 22
   Mind Versus Brain 22
   What Is Psychology And Mental Health? 25
   The Origins Of Psychology 26
   What Is Mental Health? 28
   Contributing Factors And Symptoms 29

CHAPTER 2: Warning Signs Of Mental Illness 32

   Psychological 33
   Physical 34
   Other Symptoms May Include 35

CHAPTER 3: THE EFFECTS OF STRESS ON THE MIND AND BODY 39

   Types Of Stress And Harmful Effects 39
   Managing Stress 41
   IMPACT OF COVID-19 AND LOCKDOWN 44

CHAPTER 4: WOMEN AND CHILDREN'S MENTAL HEALTH: SPECIAL CASE STUDIES 47

Perinatal Depression 48
Premenstrual Dysphoric Disorder 50
THE SPECIAL NEEDS OF MINORS WITH MENTAL ILLNESS 51

CHAPTER 5: 59

DEFINITION OF CHRISTIANITY 59

What Is Christianity? 59
The Ten Commandments 62
Nine Elements Of The Christian Faith 63
Christian Faith In Action Across The Globe 69

CHAPTER 6: THE CHRISTAIN FAITH Vs. MEDICINE/HEALTH 71

Understanding The Dichotomy 71
The Role Of The Church 75

CHAPTER 7: STEREOTYPES AND MISCONCEPTIONS ABOUT MENTAL HEALTH AMONG CHURCH MEMBERS 78

How To Counter Stereotypes Surrounding Mental Illness In The Church 91

CHAPTER 8: UNDERSTANDING THE MIND OF CHRIST IN RELATION TO MENTAL HEALTH .. 99

   The Biblical Perspective 99
   How To Renew Your Mind 108

CHAPTER 9: MENTAL ILLNESS AND AVAILABLE TREATMENTS 111

   Pharmacological And Non-Pharmacological Treatments 111

CHAPTER 10: THE MENTAL HEALTH RESOURCES AVAILABLE TO CHRISTIANS 118

   Mental Health Charities 118
   Church Of England Resources 122
   Other Agencies And Resources 123
   Resources For Young People 125

CHAPTER 11: THE POWER OF HABITS 126

   MAINTAINING GOOD MENTAL HEALTH 133
   MANAGING THE BUSYNESS OF LIFE: DISTRACTORS THAT AFFECT YOUR MENTAL HEALTH 135

References 139

Foreword

There are some books written for a particular season and there are some written for all times; this excellent literary work is definitely one for all times. Dr. Glory Elofuke, who my wife and I are most privileged to have worked with in the Christian ministry has been specially graced to bring this much needed resource to the Christian community at such a time as this.

Out of the many areas of need in mental health discussions, the knowledge gap is the one that requires a great deal of attention and the author has done an amazing job of addressing it. The scope of knowledge covered and the breadth of information made available in this book will meet the needs of beginners, right up to the intermediate level.

The best part of the book is its holistic approach. It addresses the sufferer, the susceptible, the immediate support group and the church leadership.

It is a call to action for all. The time and dare we say, the good life lost to mental illness compel us to do what is right when it comes to mental health matters. How many young people shall we watch have their future blighted by conditions that answers have been provided for by the providence of our good heavenly Father?

Glory Elofuke has essentially stripped the veil off the issue of mental illness in the Christian community. This she has done, not from a depressing accusatory angle but from a gentle but firm position of graciousness that is typical of her, as a loving wife, mother and caring member of the Christian community.

Every section has been carefully researched making the book a reliable and accurate source of information and guide. If this wonderful book just helps to bring down the monster of stigmatization with its resultant exacerbation of the mental health problem, then a great deal of good would have been done for the individual Christian and the gospel of our dear Lord Jesus Christ.

The author is uniquely qualified to write this book because of her strong experience as a general medical practitioner and her passionate role as a Christian leader in worship and evangelism.

It is on these two-pronged experience of secular medical work and Christian spiritual endowment that the strength of this great book is founded. It is the same wealth that the Lord blessed me with as He called me into pastoral work about twenty years ago, after spending almost two decades in medical practice.

I hereby wholeheartedly commit this book to the reader, trusting that the healing and health that the Sovereign Lord gives freely will be the daily experience of everyone. Amen.

Dr. Chris Gbenle

Pastor in Charge of Scotland Province of Redeemed Christian Church of God (RCCG)

INTRODUCTION

The Christian walk is most certainly a fulfilling one, yet it is not a walk in the park. Life's journey is froth with ups and downs; our personal experiences are convincing proofs. Nevertheless, with the right resource, knowledge and guidance by the Holy Spirit, victory is assured.

This begs the question, when you are in Christ, do things get any easier? The short answer is yes. Though the twists and turns may remain, you do not negotiate them all alone. His presence is the anchor in choppy seas, the all-knowing, all-powerful company that makes all the difference.

Zachariah 4:6 says,

"...but it is not by our power or by might, but by the spirit says the lord" (NLT).

Therefore, we can do nothing by ourselves. It takes reliance on the Holy Spirit, the one who guides and makes the way for us, to sail through the storms of life successfully. A functioning relationship and willingness to be led are prerequisites for this to happen. Isaiah 1:19 says, *"If you are willing and obedient, you will eat the good things of the land"* (NIV).

It is a given that we will be challenged in this world. Jesus said,

"If anyone would come after me, let him deny himself and take up his cross and follow me. For whoever would save his life will lose it, but whoever loses his life…" Matthew 16:24-26 (ESV).

The cross is quite unpleasant; it could signify any hardship, difficulties or challenges that life throws at us. It is quite easy to be crushed under their weight.

Encounters with life's deep waters, rivers of difficulty and fires of oppression are a matter of when, not if. Isaiah 43:2 (NLT) says,

"When you go through deep waters, I will be with you. When you go through rivers of difficulty, you will not drown. When you walk through the fire of oppression, you will not be burned up; the flames will not consume you".

The loss of a loved one, broken relationships and financial hardships are deep waters set to drown our hopes and aspirations. That co-worker keeps testing you and all you want to do is punch them in the face but Jesus said to turn the other cheek.

You try to do things the right way but for some reason, those who cheat their way through life seem to be doing better than you. From this nadir, it is easy for you to think of yourself as the fool.

Amid these, as prey, our mental health can be threatened. Under the weight of stress and anxiety, the Christian can also fall into depression. Elijah was a fervent prophet who boldly confronted the Prophets of Baal and closed the heavens to rain, yet he too experienced a season of depression, wishing for death. Christians face challenges and persecutions. Even Jesus who was fully God, clothe in our humanity, cried in the face of grief (John 11:35 *"...Jesus Wept" (KJV)*)

So, when you are at life's lowest ebb, when it seems like no one understands, what do you do? Who do you turn to?

It may feel like God does not get it, but He does and His word is a life hack especially if you are struggling with mental health issues. He knows all. He sees all. He is there, always ready to help. All you have to do is open your heart and let Him in.

Mental health has become an important issue in the last few years. For centuries, it was a taboo subject.

Now it has become a topic for social media platforms and fora. Employers are talking about it and developing innovative health programs to help employees. Family members are discussing it at the dinner table and Television shows now include characters with depression or bipolar disorder.

So what does this hot trend mean if you are a Christian? Should the pastor initiate a dialogue with a church member separately? There are so many questions and very few answers, unless you know where to look: the Bible.

Mental illness is not new to Christians. They already know that Jesus cast out demons. The Apostles had their "personality quirks" and personal issues to overcome or accept as a part of life. King Saul lost his mind, surely the woman who hemorrhaged for twelve years had bouts of depression as perhaps did Job, who begged God to let him die.

Fear is mentioned numerous times in the Bible whether as simply sadness or debilitating worry and anxiety. Most believers misinterpret scriptures about fear like *1 Chronicles 28:20 (KJV) – "And David said to Solomon his son, Be strong and of good courage, and do it: fear not, nor be dismayed: for the Lord God, even my God, will be with thee…"* It does not mean that you should not *feel* fear, rather it means that you should not run from the fear you feel.

Perhaps the biggest benefit of learning about mental health is self-awareness. Knowledge about the parts of the brain that are most affected by a mental illness will help you understand what you are experiencing.

This book will help Christians learn how to manage their mental health by relying on God and His word. As you learn the facts about mental health, your appreciation for God's word will grow. Confusion will be greatly reduced as you become aware of your options. Your mental illness will probably not cease to exist, but you do not have to be its victim. As Christians, we are overcomers – *John 5:4 (NKJV) says "For whatsoever is born of God overcomes the world…"*

You will also discover the history of psychology and mental health as well as be able to trace its steps leading up till the present (2021). You will understand how Sigmund Freud, Carl Jung and other notable psychologists influenced the science of the mind and behavior.

The method of research for this book was reading the Bible, scholarly journals, books and research studies. Mental health blogs and websites were also visited.

CHAPTER 1:
A DEEP DIVE

Why Mental Health?

The purpose of this book is to draw attention to mental health and share its essence from my perspective as a medical professional and practicing Christian.

Over the years and in my experience as a GP (General Practitioner) working with people experiencing mental health related issues (depression, schizophrenia, anxiety), I have found that it cuts across racial, religious and other demographic lines. For some Christians and ethnicities, mental health can be a taboo subject.

Now, let us explore one of the most important questions this book intends to answer:

Does mental health matter? Statistics show that:

- Mental health diagnoses are one of the leading causes of overall disease burden globally with 792 million people affected by mental health issues.

- This and other behavioural problems account for 40 million years of disability in 20 to 29 year olds worldwide.
- Globally, major depression is the second leading cause of disability and a significant contributor to the burden of suicide and coronary artery disease (Heart Attacks).
- According to the Adult Psychiatric mobility survey (2014) in England, it is estimated that 1 in 6 people had a common mental health disorder (Female - 1 in 5; Male - 1 in 8).
- In England alone, the cost of mental ill-health is estimated at £105billion per year.
- 70 to 75% of people with diagnosable mental illnesses do not receive any treatment at all. This is worse among ethnic minority groups.
- According to a publication in the Lancet (Global Health) 2020, 80% of individuals with serious mental health needs cannot access care in Nigeria.
- Nearly 13% of young people (5 to 19 years) had at least one mental health disorder on assessment (Mental Health of children and young people in England 2017).

- Mental disorders also shorten lives. According to the WHO, Life expectancy in severe mental health disorder is reduced by 10 to 25 years.
- Suicide is not a secret. The National Center for Health Statistics reported that, "in 2018, there were 48,344 recorded suicides." Before the COVID-19 pandemic, celebrities like Anthony Bourdain and Kate Spade committed suicide. These two deaths caused a heightened awareness about an age-old illness.

The nature and extent of human suffering linked to mental illness is huge and tells a bigger tale than just the statistics. Behind these numbers are traumatized, wounded and befuddled lives. They are often torn apart internally and socially isolated from their families and communities.

The indications and symptoms of mental disease are numerous and varied. They touch on the very essence of our human experience. It cuts to the core of our sense of self and perception of the world around us. If we can no longer rely on our own ability to find meaning in what we encounter, remember our own past or rely on our own convictions in what is real, the resultant effect is that life becomes dominated by worry and a sense hopelessness.

Generally, in many societies, it is those who have the least that suffer the most. Stigma, bullying, prejudice and social exclusion are all linked to mental health issues. This is both a cause and effect situation. So, for example, being stigmatized for any reason increases the likelihood of mental disorders but being diagnosed or labelled as mentally ill is associated with even more stigma. This has an impact on every aspect of life.

Regardless of the statistics, the issue of mental health has been relegated to the background even in the Christian community, where care and love should be exemplary. A lot of people do not talk about mental health issues, neither do they understand or recognize the importance.

Let us correct that:

Mental health revolves around our emotions and psychology as human beings. Therefore, whatever tampers with the sanctity of our emotional and psychological mind-set affects our mental health. In more plain terms, anything that affects our mental health affects how we reason, process information and react. They are the reasons we do what we do and they dictate how we handle situations like stress, loss and interpersonal relationships.

At this point, it is glaring that mental health is extremely important because while most people focus mainly on physical health, mental health can be the engine that fuels physical activities and the choices we make.

HOW THE MIND WORKS

If you are a Christian dealing with depression, anxiety, bipolar disorder or any other psychological condition, you may have wondered about how your mind works at some point. Of course, you are not the first person to ask that question. It may help to know about psychologists who have wondered about the same issues and provided evidence-based answers. So this section will introduce you to basic psychological and mental health principles.

Mind versus Brain

The mind is referred to as human consciousness. It can be defined as your set of intellectual faculties. The mind is a group of cognitive psychiatric processes. It functions using perception, memory and reasoning.

> Attention: The ability to focus and concentrate on specific stimuli. It is a cognitive process that makes it possible for you to react to stimuli.

> Perception: This is the ability to capture and process data related to your five senses. It interprets your surroundings with the things around you through sensory organs.

> Memory: Your brain's ability to retain information is based on memory. You can recover information at will. Memory makes it possible to retrieve facts, concepts, feelings, etc.

> Reasoning: Cognitive functions like reasoning can be learned. They make it possible to relate the information that you are aware of, with information stored. This connection helps you hypothesize facts. This is needed for problem solving.

> Coordination: A collaboration between your mind, brain and bodily functions is needed to move efficiently. It is this function that helps you interact with the world around you.

The National Institute of Health published an article titled, "The Brain and Child Development: Time for

Some Critical Thinking". This article highlighted these facts about cognitive skills and the brain:

1. Since the late 1970s, neuroscientists have discovered that rats, cats and primates experience a period of fast synapse (small pocket of space between cells where messages are passed) development. A single neuron can contain thousands of synapses. It happens in the cortex. During this time, nerve cells form prior to birth or soon after.
2. Periods of experience-dependent development in some sensory and motor systems. For animals, a deprivation of visual stimulation results in permanent blindness.
3. Researchers proved that enriched environments increase brain size, weight and number of synapses per cortical neuron.

These facts illustrate the fact that in humans, the period of rapid synopsis development ends around the age of three. However, between childhood and adulthood, the brain loses excess neurons and synapses are reduced. By the time you enter your twenties, the rate of loss decreases.

Simultaneously, some parts of the brain gain strength by making connections. The major nerve tracts are wrapped in myelin that acts as a protective covering. It increases the brain's white matter and this area reaches peak performance at age of forty.

The brain has three main parts: cerebrum, cerebellum and brainstem. The cerebrum is the largest part. It has the left and right hemispheres. It is responsible for interpreting touch, vision and hearing. It also controls speech, reasoning and even emotions.

The cerebral cortex is made of billions of neurons and glial cells that provide support to the nervous system. It is separated into four lobes. The frontal lobe is for thinking and planning. Memory and judgment also occur in this area.

What is Psychology and Mental Health?

According to the American Psychological Association, Psychology is the scientific study of the mind and behavior. It is a complex topic with many facets and specific disciplines, e.g. child psychology, criminal psychology and abnormal psychology.

The origins of psychology can be traced to ancient Greece, about 400–500 years ago. During that time, psychology was considered a philosophical endeavor. Some of the world's best thinkers like Socrates (470 BC – 399 BC), Plato (428 BC – 348 BC) and Aristotle (384 BC – 322 BC) influenced psychology. These philosophers discussed memory, free will, determinism and nature versus nurture.

The Origins of Psychology

Wilhelm Wundt is considered the Father of Psychology. He was a notable psychologist from 1832 to 1920. Wundt was a pioneer who separated psychology from philosophy. He analyzed the structure of the mind and emphasized an objective measurement. He discovered Structuralism, a breaking down of mental processes into parts. It is based on introspection, a research method where subjects related to what was happening in their minds while simultaneously performing a task.

Wundt opened the Institute for Experimental Psychology (IEP), the first laboratory dedicated to psychology, at the University of Leipzig in Germany in 1879. The opening of the institute is considered as the beginning of modern psychology.

Wundt studied reaction times and sensory process. The school of psychology that Wundt founded is referred to as voluntarism. It is the process of organizing the mind. He wanted to study the structure of the human mind by using introspection. He believed in reductionism - that consciousness could be broken down to its basic parts. Wundt's greatest contribution to the field was the proof that psychology was a valid experimental science.

Five Notable Psychologists		
	Name	Discoveries
1	Sigmund Freud (1856-1939)	Austrian neurologist and founder of psychoanalysis, theory of the human psyche. Discovered the unconscious mind.
2	B. F. Skinner (1904-1990)	Founder of Behaviorism – human action result of conditioning, not free will.
3	Jean Piaget (1896 – 1980)	First psychologist to make a systematic study of cognitive development.

4	Ivan Pavlov (1849 – 1936)	Known for his study of classical conditioning and experiment referred to as Pavlov's Dog and the digestive system of dogs that salivated for food.
5	Carl Jung (1875 – 1961)	Developed concepts about introvert and extrovert personality types, archetypes and the collective unconscious.

What is Mental Health?

According to the World Health Organization, "mental health is a state of well-being in which the individual realizes his or her own abilities, can cope with the normal stresses of life, can work productively and fruitfully and is able to make a contribution to his or her community".

Mental health also includes emotional and psychological well-being. Good mental health has a social aspect as well. People need to connect with other people in order to be healthy. Stress can affect your mental health. Mental health is important at every stage of life. Even children should have good mental health.

Contributing Factors and Symptoms

Over the course of your life, your needs will change. If you experience a difference in your thinking, mood and behavior, it could indicate a mental health issue. Some other signs are as follows:

> **Biological Factors**

Your genes or Neurochemistry can affect how you feel. Biological psychology (also called physiological psychology) is the study of the effect of biology on behavior. It is concerned with the nervous system, hormones and genetics. It examines the connection between the mind and body by considering the influence of the brain, immune system and nervous system. Genetics is also a major factor.

> **Life Experiences**

The Center for Anxiety Disorders defines trauma as "a psychological emotional response to an event or experience that is deeply distressing or disturbing". Trauma can make you perceive things that trigger memories or painful events as threats. Some examples of trauma include physical or sexual abuse, childhood abandonment, bullying, death of a loved one, stress suffered by first responders or veterans and substance abuse or addiction. A traumatic event we had to endure due to lapses in parenting can make a lifelong mark that shapes how we react to the outside world. The scars of a sexual assault in childhood for example could close the doors of marital openness and trust among other ills.

> **Family History of Mental Health Conditions**

Scientific research has shown that having family members with depression, anxiety, bipolar disorder, schizophrenia, etc. increases your risk. Of course, genetics may make you more vulnerable. For instance, a brain scan can reveal over activity in a specific part of the brain for all members of the family. If you were raised in a stressful environment, then the likelihood of developing depression or any other mental illness is increased. American Addiction Centers said, "Having a parent that suffers from alcohol abuse issues may deeply and profoundly impact your development and overall life".

CHAPTER 2:

Warning Signs of Mental Illness

Major mental illnesses such as schizophrenia or bipolar disorder rarely appear "out of the blues". Most often, relatives, friends, teachers or individuals themselves begin to observe little changes or a sense that "something is not quite right" about their thinking, feelings or behaviour before an illness appears in its full-blown form.

Learning about developing symptoms or early warning signs and taking the necessary action can help. Early intervention can reduce the severity of an illness. It may even be possible to delay or prevent a major mental illness altogether.

Many people today, believers and non-believers alike live their lives unaware that their symptoms or feelings are harbingers of mental health diagnosis. Like physical illness, symptoms of mental health problems can evolve, sometimes starting small and slow. The routine of a busy life gets in the way. We procrastinate talking to family or visiting that GP for a quick chat. Inevitably it all gets too much and overwhelms us over time.

This section is focused on creating awareness of subtle and not-so-subtle signs of some common mental problems encountered in the society today. It is not to alarm you but to empower you to seek help and support from professionals.

Here are some of the warning signs associated with mental illnesses:

Psychological

Mood Swings — Rapid changes in moods often affecting relationships. One moment you feel happy and joyful and the next, you are feeling deeply sad. This may be a sign of mental illness and is worth consulting your doctor for.

Withdrawal — This involves social withdrawal and isolation out with the occasional desire for a quiet place to get things done. Generally keeping to one's self and shunning interaction with even close family contacts.

Decline in all round performance — when there is an unusual drop in normal functioning e.g. at school, work or other social activities. You may quit a once loved sport and struggle with performing familiar tasks.

Incoherent thoughts or ideas and new beliefs outside social norms - This may involve problems with concentration and expressing logical thoughts. Harboring ideas of a persecutory nature or those that confers one with superhuman powers. These would normally be outside the boundaries of known religious / social beliefs.

Feeling disconnected — a vague feeling of being disconnected from oneself or your surroundings or a sense of unreality. You often feel like you are in another plane of existence, disconnected from the rest of the world and things around you. You have no interest in the news, sports or things happening in your immediate environment.

Nervousness — a feeling that impending doom ensues. One feels fear and nervousness that cannot be explained and gets paranoid easily.

Physical

Sleep and appetite changes - Sleep and good nutrition are key to your mental and physical wellbeing. Dramatic sleep and appetite changes (binge eating or food avoidance) are common in a variety of mental health disorders including anxiety, depression, bipolar disorder and substance misuse.

Feeling tired all the time- Whilst this can be explained by physical illness, it is not an uncommon sign of mental health problems. The lack of energy and fatigue is often unexplained and has adverse effects on activities of daily living.

Other symptoms may include

- Having aches and pains without a physical cause
- Feeling numb or indifferent
- Giving up hope and feeling powerless
- Feeling unusually confused, forgetful, or anxious
- irritability
- Hearing voices or believing things that are not true
- Self-destructive thoughts that include harming yourself or others

- Inability to perform daily tasks like attending to basic hygiene, taking care of your children,
- or going to work.

All these signs are by no means exhaustive. They are commonplace among many and should be used only as a trigger for action. They are not mutually exclusive either. If you or a loved one experience any of these symptoms persistently, I recommend talking about it and seeking professional help. You may be tempted to handle the situation alone. However, that usually makes it worse. Isolation feeds negativity, so talk with your family or friends about your experiences. Consider the following suggestions:

1. **Live your life on your own terms**

    Realize your full potential regarding education, career, and relationships. The pressure to conform can be a driver of social and personal insecurities that perpetuate stress and anxiety. Therefore, resist the pressure to conform to negative stereotypes

Fads, and trends if they do not validate your personal principles or genuinely make you happy and at peace. Accept counsel but do not live-in other people's shadows.

2. **Manage Stress**

   Stress or anxiety is usually a part of trying something new. Devise a plan of how you will overcome it. Exercise including cardiovascular and strength training can help with fitness and also contribute to a positive outlook and control anxiety. Get enough sleep, usually 6 to 8 hours.

3. **Work Productivity**

   Do you have a plan for how you will handle the demands of your job, school and family responsibilities? You must be realistic and develop a strategy. Ask for help from others and manage your time wisely.

4. **Contribution to Society**

Are you a part of a group at school, work or your church? Collaborating with other people helps you discuss your emotions, ideas, etc. Group involvement helps you serve your community and promotes a feeling of achievement.

5. **Christian Counseling**

    This is a combination of <u>theology</u> and psychology, delivered by a Christian psychologist. As you would expect, it explains the human mind and behavior while adhering to biblical principles. As the Bible says in Proverbs 11:14 (KJV), *"Where there is no counsel, the people fall; but in the multitude of counselors there is safety"*.

CHAPTER 3:
THE EFFECTS OF STRESS ON THE MIND AND BODY

Types of Stress and Harmful Effects

The National Institutes of Health, in its article titled, "Traumatic Stress: effect on the Brain", said, "Brain areas implicated in the stress response include the amygdala, hippocampus and prefrontal cortex." Furthermore, "Traumatic stress can be associated with lasting changes in these brain areas". Everyone has experienced stress in their lives, it is the way the brain and body react to a demand. However, the Bible says in *John 14:1 (NIV) "Do not let your heart be troubled. You believe in God; believe also in me"*.

Good and Bad Types of Psychological Stress

Stress is a feeling of emotional strain. Bad stress can take the form of resentment, fears, frustration, grief, jealously, self-loathing and even cognitive stress (information overload). Psychosocial stress can manifest as problems in relationships.

Other causes of stress are based on a feeling of deficiency or shortage such as lack of resources for survival, loss of loves ones, bankruptcy and isolation. <u>Psycho-spiritual</u> stress occurs when there is a crisis of values and purpose. Striving to achieve something, but being unable to find joy or satisfaction in the journey or attainment can be stressful.

However, stress could also be positive. Positive stress helps improve performance. In a dangerous situation, stress signals the body to "fight or flight". This term means that during a stressful time, your body pumps more adrenaline and you breathe faster, your muscles become tense and your brain requires more oxygen. It may be a one-time occurrence or a lengthy situation. Some people are more resilient than others. Examples include:

- Everyday pressures related to job or school performance;
- Stress caused by a sudden change such as job loss, death or divorce;
- Traumatic stress experienced during an event such as an accident, war, natural disaster or sexual assault.

Of course, negative stress can affect your health. Long-term stress can damage your health. Chronic stress is difficult to manage. Due to the fact that the source of long-term stress is almost continual compared to acute stress, the body does not receive a clear signal to return to normal. With Chronic stress, the same lifesaving reactions in the body can affect the immune system, digestive, cardiovascular, sleep and reproductive systems negatively. Most people are aware of stress in their digestive system because they experience queasiness or loss of appetite and irritable bowel. Other people react to stress with a headache, insomnia, sadness or irritability.

Over time, you either ignore the signs of stress in your body because you get used to it. So the lingering stress contributes to serious health issues like heart disease, high blood pressure and diabetes. Depression and anxiety can also result from stress.

Managing Stress

Stress can be handled properly. Here are some recommendations for handling stress:

➢ **Be Vigilant to Body Signs**

Recognize the signs of your body's response to stress. Problems with sleep, alcohol or drug use, irritation and low energy are symptoms of stress.

➢ **Exercise Regularly**

An exercise routine does not have to be a strenuous workout. Start with low-impact routines like bending and stretching. Take long walks, dance, swim or play golf. Set a schedule and stick to it. There will be more discussion about exercise in subsequent chapters of this book.

➢ **Set Goals and Priorities**

Create a To-Do list and decide what is important and what can wait. Consider using the Four Quadrants of Time Management. Focus more on what you achieved and its long-term effects as opposed to what you did not achieve.

> **Rely on Family and Friends**

    Personal relationships have been shown to have a positive effect on your health. "People who have strong social relationships are less likely to die prematurely than people who are isolated," said an article published by Live Science in 2016. Family and friends offer emotional support. They can also help you reach your goals, so engage in conversations and do not be afraid to ask for help.

The Next Generation of Stress

Most parents do not know that the stress they experience could affect their children's health as well. A new field of genetics called Epigenetics refers to the study of how your behaviors and environment can cause changes that affect the way your genes work. This reveals that our habits and emotions can impact our biology to the extent that it causes changes in the genes that are carried over to several generations. So the stress related with the mental health challenges in your parents, grandparents, or great-grandparents have actually been changed. This mutation means they are more vulnerable to health issues.

However, according to the Centers for Disease Control and Prevention, the good news is that "Unlike genetic changes, epigenetic changes are reversible and do not change your DNA sequence, but they can change how your body reads a DNA sequence".

IMPACT OF COVID-19 AND LOCKDOWN

The Effects of Covid-19 on Mental Health

Although the public health measures for fighting COVID-19 were valid, the quarantine was especially difficult for people with a mental illness. According to the International Journal of Mental Health's article titled "Life in the Pandemic: Social Isolation and Mental Health", "Isolation is known to cause psychosocial problems, especially for those recognized as vulnerable. While all humans are at risk of psychosocial harm when kept in isolation, the most vulnerable in these situations are children…minority groups…and people with pre-existing mental health conditions."

In addition to the effects of stress mentioned previously, COVID-19 added another layer of complexity. All of the sudden, you are forced to cope with working from home, learning new technology, home-schooling the children and limited contact with friends and family. Also, you had to deal with the ever-looming possibility of contracting a deadly virus.

So how do Christians with a mental illness cope? Here are some helpful tips:

1. **Limit watching the news or reading stories**

    According to the Centers for Disease Control and Prevention, "It is good to be informed, but hearing about the pandemic constantly can be upsetting". Limit the time you spend hearing about <u>COVID-19 updates</u> via <u>watching television,</u> surfing the web or listening to the news on any device.

2. **Talk with people (church members)**

    While social distance measures are in place, most places of worship have streaming services and have opened their social media space so that members can connect. *Hebrews 10:25 (NKJV) says "...not forsaking the assembling of ourselves together, as is the manner of some, but exhorting one another and so much the more as ye see the Day approaching".*

3. **Pray**

1 Thessalonians 5:17 (NKJV) says *"Pray without ceasing"*. Praying is one of the most powerful things you can do. It is a demonstration of your faith in God, not in your own strength. A fervent prayer is needed as mentioned in James 5:16 (NIV) *"Therefore confess your sins to each other and pray for each other so that you may be healed. The prayer of a righteous person is powerful and effective"*.

4. **Rely on God's Promises**

   Because of Jesus, you can be assured that you will spend eternity in God's presence. As a believer, your future is promising. *John 14:3 (NKJV) "And if I go and prepare a place for you, I will come again and receive you to myself; that where I am, there you may be also"*.

CHAPTER 4:

WOMEN AND CHILDREN'S MENTAL HEALTH: SPECIAL CASE STUDIES

Women and men can be affected by mental health issues differently. According to BMJ 2016; 354:i5320), Depression and Anxiety are more common in Women than in Men. So a Christian woman must put her faith in God. As Proverbs 31:30 (ESV) says, *"Charm is deceitful and beauty is vain, but a woman that fears the Lord is to be praised"*.

According to the National Institutes of Health, "there are also certain types of disorders that are unique to women". Women may experience symptoms of mental disorders at times of hormonal change. Perinatal depression, premenstrual dysphoric disorder and perimenopause-related depression are examples of mental health disorders associated with hormonal changes in women.

Perinatal Depression

Perinatal depression (PD) is a mood disorder that occurs during or after pregnancy. Symptoms could occur during the pregnancy (also referred to as pregnancy depression) or the depression begins after the baby arrives(Postnatal depression). Symptoms include extreme sadness, anxiety, fatigue, frequent crying, changes in appetite and loss of interest in leisure activities or hobbies. Most notably, is the inability to feel connected with the child. Some women experience hallucinations or think about harming themselves or the baby. PD may interfere with the mother's performance of routine duties like caring for herself or the baby.

According to the National Institutes of Health, "perinatal depression is real medical illness that can affect any mother". Age, race, income, culture, etc. does not matter. Women are not to blame for PD. It is not based on anything the mother has done. It does not have a specific cause. PD is based on a combination of factors like genetics and the environment. Life stress as well as the physical and emotional demands for caring for an infant can contribute to its development.

It is estimated that between 10 and 20 percent of women develop some type of pregnancy-related mood disorder. Also, 1 in 20 women in the United States of America (USA) will have a major depressive disorder while expecting their babies. Women are at greater risk if they have personal or family history of depression or bipolar disorder or if they experienced PD with a previous pregnancy.

Another condition that affects women is postpartum depression. Postpartum depression is different from "baby blues". Baby blues describes mood changes, feelings of anxiety and sadness. Many women also experience exhaustion in the first two weeks after the baby is born. Babies require twenty four hour care. Baby blues are considered severe if it continues after two weeks. Women with postpartum depression usually require a doctor's care.

If you are a woman experiencing PD, speak with your GP, midwife or other healthcare provider. Treatment options include therapy and various medications that are safe during the pregnancy and while breastfeeding.

Premenstrual dysphoric disorder

Premenstrual dysphoric disorder (PMDD) is a disabling extension of premenstrual syndrome. It includes physical and behavioral signs that usually resolve with the onset of menstruation. It is very common and affects about three million women in the United States of America (U.S.A) per year.

Self-care includes exercise and stress management. Cognitive behavioral therapy and medications like birth control and antidepressants are also helpful.

Pre-menopause-related depression

In some cases of menopause, the reduction of estrogen can cause issues with mental illness. Peri-menopausal depression can cause chronic anxiety and distress during a certain time of the month.

Hormones are the messengers in the body that can determine the rate of chemical functions. Hormones can maintain, stop or slow down functions. Ovaries are the source of estrogen and progesterone. Other symptoms include night sweats, stress, difficulty concentrating and lack of motivation.

THE SPECIAL NEEDS OF MINORS WITH MENTAL ILLNESS

Deuteronomy 6:7 (NKJV) – "You shall teach them diligently to your children, and shall talk of them when you sit in your house, when you walk by the way, when you lie down and when you rise up".

Detecting Mental Illness in Children

God loves children. *Jeremiah 1:5 says "Before I formed you in the womb I knew you, and before you were born I set you apart and appointed you as a prophet to the nations"* (Berean Study Bible). God is always concerned about their health and safety. In Mark 5:22 – 43, Jesus brought back to life a twelve year old girl that was dead.

When Jesus walked the earth, there was little or no mention of children and teens with mental illnesses, but no doubt, they existed. Today children and adolescents with a mental illness are common. Consider these statistics provided by the Mental

Health Foundation, the United Kingdom's leading charity for mental health:

> Mental health problems affect around <u>one in six children</u>. They include depression, anxiety and conduct disorder (a type of behavioral problem) and are often a direct response to what is happening in their lives.

> Alarmingly, however, 75% of children and young people who experience a mental health problem are not getting the help they need.

According to an article, "Annotation: Pathways to care for children with mental health Problems", children with mental health problems do not receive the care they need by their primary health care provider. <u>Children with mental health</u> usually exhibit signs. Parents should be keenly aware of symptoms because it is the first step to getting the help the child needs.

Most children have a primary care doctor. Parents know that besides physical injuries, psychological issues should also be discussed, but few children demonstrate symptoms, even if their parents suspect something is wrong. Less than 50% of children with disorders are recognized by their doctor. If the child is recognized with a disorder, only half are referred to a specialist. Up to 33% receive professional treatment for a mental health service provider.

The type of disorder and its severity is a major factor. Also, the child's age, gender and social backgrounds can contribute to the illness.

Predictably, the <u>pandemic</u> has affected children with mental health including young people of colour. Since parents had reported higher stress levels, so did their children. Children's risk of family adversity increased the likelihood of child abuse and neglect as well as domestic violence.

Experts conclude that there are discrepancies in the patterns of service. Barriers involving the perception of the parents and expressions of concerns within consultations should be addressed. Efforts should be made to minimize anything that could interfere with treatment. Public education methods and training as well as support from the mental health specialists and doctors should be enhanced.

Physical Illness Affecting Children and Adolescents with Mental Health

The World Health Organization reported that, "One in six people aged <u>10 to 19 years</u> have mental health conditions accounting for 16% of the global burden of disease and injury in people 10 to 19 years". Also, about 50% of all mental health conditions start before the age of 15. However, most cases are not detected and therefore not treated.

The most common mental illnesses in adolescents are anxiety, mood and attention disorders. Experts also say behavior disorders are disruptive behavior that lasts for at least six months. These conditions cause problems in school and at home. Suicide is the second leading cause of death in young adults from 15 to 24 years.

<u>Physical illness</u> can affect children's mental health. In "Psychological Adjustment and Asthma in Children and Adolescents: The UK Nationwide Mental Health Survey," this phenomenon was proven. It said, "Children with asthma appear to be at increased risk of behavioral and emotional problems. This appears to be particularly the case for internalizing problems, which include anxiety and depression". Doctors observed different causal factors including socioeconomic, demographic, family, factors etc.

The majority of studies examining the correlation between psychosocial and physical factors have been conducted on clinic-recruited children with asthma. Also, some prospective studies focus on children at high biological risk of developing symptoms. Some studies involving medication have suggested that the administration of certain types of corticosteroids may influence hyperactivity. The study said, "in contrast, a large-scale multicenter trial of children with mild to moderate asthma indicated no elevation in neurocognitive difficulty."

The asthma may not be the factor that results in higher ratings of mental problems, but the children who were sick or whose asthma presented strongly are at a higher risk for mental health issues. If poorly controlled, they are at particular risk of being reported as having psychological difficulties. Children presenting poor psychological management had chronic illnesses, faulty functional status, and more school absences. So to the extent that the child is sick parallels their ability to adjust psychologically.

Adolescent Treatment versus Adult Treatment for Mental Health Illness

Adolescents experience mental illness differently from adults. Look at the figures and it is obvious. Consider the following data provided by Substance Abuse and

Mental Health Services Administration (SAMHSA), Center for Behavioral Health Statistics and Quality (May 6, 2014):

- Approximately 938,000 U.S.A adolescents aged 16 to 17 years had major depressive episode (MDE) in the past year. This represents one out of every ten older adolescents in the country.
- Older adolescents (aged 16 or 17 years) were more likely than younger adolescents (aged 12 to 15 years) to have had MDE in the past year.
- About 214,000 older adolescents (3.1 %) had co-occurring MDE and substance use disorder (SUD) in the past year.
- Nearly three quarters of adolescents aged 16 to 17 years with MDE were female.

Children and adolescents with a mental illness have a poorer quality of life than those without a mental illness. In the U.S.A., adolescents that are over 15 years old begin to transition into adulthood. It continues into their mid-20s. As these young people grow up, they make pivotal decisions about education, careers and relationships. If you have schizophrenia, substance use disorder (SUD) or another other mental disorder, this time in your life can be especially difficult. According to Substance Abuse and Mental Health Services Administration (SAMHSA) "Studies have shown that there is nearly a twofold increase in mood disorders in the 13-to-14-year-old-age group than in the 17-to-18-year-old age group."

As stated previously, clinical interventions can reduce mental health illnesses. The *Journal of American Medical Association* (JAMA Pediatrics) published "Treatment Options for <u>Adolescent Depression</u>." Medical experts said, "Not all therapy is the same. A type of therapy called cognitive behavioral therapy has strong evidence that it can help your child learn their depressive thoughts and develop skills to change them." Interpersonal therapy is also effective.

Some teens may have success with antidepressants like a serotonin reuptake inhibitor (SSRIs). Serotonin is one of the chemical messengers (neurotransmitters) that send signals between brain neurons.

CHAPTER 5:
DEFINITION OF CHRISTIANITY

What is Christianity?

Christianity is the belief in the birth, life, death and resurrection of Jesus Christ. *John 3:16 (NKJV) says "For God so loved the world that He gave His only begotten Son, that whoever believes in Him should not perish but have everlasting life".* The disciples of Jesus demonstrated His character and the people of those days recognized them as Christ-like. This was the first time in scripture 'Christian' was ever used to describe the followers of Jesus, the Christ (Acts 11:26).

In more recent years, Christianity is divided between Eastern and Western theology. These divisions include six branches that are discussed below. Restorationism is considered by some people to be the seventh branch. Within these branches, there are denominations.

Christianity is the most widely practiced religion in the world. It has more than 2 billion followers. More than 70% of people identify themselves as Christians. Sunday is regarded as the holy day of the week.

Followers should rest on the seventh day just as God did after he created the world *(Genesis 2:2)*.

Christianity has six main branches:

- ➤ **Catholicism** – About half of all Christians are Catholics. Catholics believe in the unity of body and soul. The Census of the 2020 Annuario Pontificio reported that the number of baptized Catholics was 1.459 billion. In the U.S.A, there are about 70 million Catholics representing 22% of the population.

- ➤ **Protestantism** – A member of the Western Christian churches, but separate from the Roman Catholic Church, the largest Christian church. Baptists are a major branch of Protestant Christianity. Some Christians believe that there has been a continuation of Baptist churches from the time of John the Baptist and the Apostles of Jesus Christ. Most experts agree that Baptists spoke English. The religion started during the 17th Century Puritanism as a sub-sect of Congregationalism. Baptists believe that baptism should include immersion, not sprinkling of water.

- **Eastern Orthodoxy** - Christians who believe in one God who is both three and one (Trinity) – the Father, Son and Holy Spirit.

  Anglican – A Western Christian tradition that grew out of the practices, liturgy, etc. of the Church of England. The archbishop of Canterbury is the highest-ranking cleric.

- **Oriental Orthodoxy** – In Ethiopia, this religion accounts for more than 40% of religions. It is the communion of Eastern Christian Churches. It acknowledges only three ecumenical councils.

  Assyrians – This religion is mostly Christian. They are followers of the East and West Syriac (language of ancient Syria) liturgical rites of Christianity.

- **Orthodox** – The origin is Greek *orthodoxos*, meaning "of the right opinion". Adherents consider it to be the true doctrine opposed to heterodox (not conforming to accepted or orthodox standards or beliefs) or heretical (having an opinion that differs from generally accepted concepts) doctrines.

> **Restorationism** – On the Christianity website, it said, "Truth can only be seen rightly 'through the lens of Jesus Christ". However, in today's world, the teachings of Jesus differs from what is taught inside and outside the Restoration Movement. Restorationists refer to 2 Corinthians 13:11 (NIV) – *"Finally, brothers and sisters, rejoice! Strive for full restoration, encourage one another…be of one mind, live in peace. And the God of love and peace will be with you."*

The Ten Commandments

Christianity has Ten Commandments or Decalogue and they are the biblical principles of God that were given to Moses. These laws relate to ethics and worship and were the foundation of Judaism and Christianity. Bible scholars disagree about when they were written. However, the book of Exodus *(Exodus 20: 1- 17)* in the Torah reveals that the Ten Commandments were given to Moses at Mount Sinai. The commandments are as follows:

1. I am the Lord thy God: thou shalt not have strange gods before me

2. Thou shall not take the name of the Lord thy God in vain

3. Remember to keep holy the Lord's Day

4. Honour thy father and thy mother

5. Thou shalt not kill

6. Thou shalt not commit adultery

7. Thou shalt not steal

8. Thou shalt not bear false witness against thy neighbour

9. Thou shalt not covet thy neighbour's wife

10. Thou shalt not covet thy neighbour's goods

God gave these laws as a guide for humans to live their lives. If followed, His people would be protected against evil. The Ten Commandments are still valid today.

Nine Elements of the Christian Faith

Here are nine elements of the Christian faith.

The Bible

The Bible is the inspired word of God. It was written by more than forty authors, through the supernatural guidance of the Holy Spirit. The Bible is the truth and without error. *2 Timothy 3:16- 17 (NKJV) says "All Scripture is given by inspiration of God and is profitable for doctrine, for reproof, for correction, for instruction in righteousness".* So it is completely relevant to your life today, regardless of who you are or the circumstances you are facing.

The Trinity

The trinity is one of the mysteries of God. *Habakkuk 1:5 (ESV) says "Look among the nations and see; wonder and be astounded. For I am doing a work in your days that you would not believe if told".* So as humans we may never fully comprehend God's ways. However, the scriptures give us insight about God. It is obvious that God wants a relationship with His family. God has always existed. He has no beginning or end.

1 John 5:7 (NKJV)-"For there are three that bear witness in heaven, the Father, the Word and the Holy Spirit, and these three are one". Each member of the Trinity has different functions. They are all equally powerful. The Trinity exists as one substance in three person: the Father, Son and Holy Spirit

The Father

God has no beginning or end. He is the great "I am." He is all things. His is omnipotent (all powerful) and omniscient (all knowing). *Matthew 19:26 (ESV) – "But Jesus looked at them and said, "With man this is impossible, but with God all things are possible".* He never sleeps and is always present (omnipresent). His love for His earthly family is unchanging. He is Holy and worthy of our love and total devotion, *Deuteronomy 6:5 (NLT) "And you must love the LORD your God with all your heart, all your soul, and all your strength".*

Jesus

Jesus Christ, the son of God, He is both completely human and God. *Luke 4:41 (NKJV) – And demons also came out of many, crying out and saying "You are the Christ the Son of God!"* However, He is the perfect man, completely God. He has a plan for bringing people who have lost their faith and sinned against God back into a right relationship with God.

His death on the cross was substitution for our deserved punishment of sin through Adam (salvation). Jesus' loving sacrifice paid our debt of sin. He defeated death through resurrection from the dead and proving to everyone that He was indeed God. He paved the way to heaven so that you could be redeemed. Also, His resurrection provided hope for all mankind and the Second Coming ensures that all God's children will be with Him in heaven.

The Holy Spirit

The Holy Spirit is the nature and power of God *(2 Timothy 1:7)*. He is a gift from God that can help the human mind to promote spiritual growth and enable a person to become a member of God's family. His presence assures us of our relationship with Christ, Romans 8:16 (NLT) *"For his Spirit joins with our spirit to affirm that we are God's children"*. The Holy Spirit draws each person to God through conviction, not condemnation. He empowers believers for holy living. Followers of Christ have special gifts that equips them for life and a strong ministry.

Christians must have the Holy Spirit. *Romans 8:9 (NLT) "But you are not controlled by your sinful nature. You are controlled by the Spirit if you have the Spirit of God living in you. (And remember that those who do not have the Spirit of Christ living in them do not belong to Him at all."*

Eternity

Man was created to live forever. All of God's children will exist either eternally separated from God by sin or in a relationship with God through the forgiveness of sin and salvation through Jesus alone. Hell is to be eternally separated from God by sin. Heaven is to be in an eternal relationship with God. Some people, mainly unbelievers, do not think that heaven and hell are real places, but the Bible makes it clear that they are eternal places of existence.

Man and His Inherited Sin

Man is made in the image of God. He is the supreme object of God's creation and love. *Genesis 2:7 – (NIV)"Then the Lord God formed man of dust from the ground and breathed into his nostrils the breath of life and man became a living being".* Man was created for God with the purpose of a thriving relationship.

Man became separated from God because of Adam's act of disobedience. Sin created a type of spiritual debt. All human beings have a sinful or carnal nature. As a result, man cannot attain a right relationship with God based on good works. *Ephesians 2:8-9 (NIV) – "For it is by grace you have been saved through faith…it is the gift of God – not by works, so that no one can boast".*

It is only through Jesus that your sins can be forgiven. Jesus's sacrifice on the cross brought those who follow Him back into right standing with the Creator.

Salvation

Jesus' sacrifice is the only payment acceptable to God. *John 3:16 (NKJV) - "For God so loved the world, that he gave His only Son, that whoever believes in Him should not perish but have everlasting life".* Jesus opened the door to repentance and forgiveness. Salvation occurs when people place their faith and trust in the death and resurrection of Christ. It is payment for sin.

The Church

The Church is referred to as the body of Christ. It consists of every person that has placed their faith in Jesus Christ. Every follower of Christ regardless of denomination or affiliation is part of the body of Christ. *Ephesians 5:24-25 (KJV) – "Therefore as the church is subject unto Christ, so let the wives be to their own husbands in everything. Husbands, love your wives, even as Christ also loved the church and gave himself for it."*

The term *church* describes a local community of believers. They are unified through faith in Christ. The church is committed to the teachings of Christ.

Believers demonstrate their faith through obedience of God's word. His followers are on a mission to preach the Gospel throughout the world.

The church is God's way of reaching the world. Members of the congregation work together in unity and love. Their mission is to glorify Christ. The church is a place where you can go exactly as you are. You do not need to be perfect. Indeed the church is a place for those who are spiritually sick and seek healing. The Holy Spirit provides sanctification. When you gather with your brothers and sisters in Christ, you get to share the message of hope in Christ.

Christian Faith in Action across the Globe

If you are a Christian struggling with a mental illness, it can seem as though you are the only person in the world experiencing sadness and despair. However, some Christians are being persecuted for their faith. Here is an inspiring story of Christians literally facing death everyday as they maintain their aliance to God.

Burma has been devastated by the COVID-19 pandemic and the ongoing violence makes the area even worse. The military took over on February 1, 2021. Some civilians have dressed like soldiers and vice versa. This makes it difficult to determine who is responsible for the damage. The locals caught in between the deadly chaos have said it is like living in a battlefield. Bombs explode day and night.

However, support from Christian Aid Mission donors has helped them with food, provisions and encouragement. The missionaries have even connected with an ethnic group that has experienced difficulties within its own tribe.

Even though Zoom church meetings are prohibited and hospitals are closed, the pastors still use Facebook to preach. Some families risk death to travel for two hours to worship together. Nevertheless, these trials have resulted with more efforts to preach the gospel and demonstrate brotherly love.

James 1:2–4 (KJV) "My brethren, count it all joy when ye fall into diverse temptations; knowing this, that the trying of your faith worketh patience. But let patience have her perfect work, that you may be perfect and entire, wanting nothing".

CHAPTER 6:
THE CHRISTAIN FAITH vs. MEDICINE/HEALTH

Understanding the Dichotomy

In this chapter, we would examine the dichotomy between Christianity and the modern field of medicine. One thing is certain, Christianity has had a major impact on medicine through empathy and care. When Jesus healed the sick, raised the dead and restored the sight of the blind in His time, He did it with so much care and love. He was moved by the challenges that these people faced.

In Luke 7:13, the bible says: *"When the Lord saw her, He felt compassion for her and He said "do not weep"* (NLT)

However, there is a flip side to the dichotomy between Christianity and modern medicine. The problem here is the understanding of what Faith is and the impact of our faith. Yes, it is great to have faith and believe in the word of God, especially when your situation is contrary to what you believe.

In fact, the Bible defined faith in Hebrews 11:1 - *"Now, faith is the assurance of things hoped for, the evidence of things not seen" (KJV)*

This means faith is to be had, despite what you are going though and even when all does not look well, believe that all is well. This is true.

Even Jesus Christ stressed the power of faith in Matthew 17: 20 "...Truly, I tell you, if you have faith like a mustard seed, you can say to this mountain, 'move from here to there and it will move..." (KJV).

It is established in the Bible that faith is powerful. However, while it is great that Christians

latch on to faith, the challenge is that we often cling on to only faith and refuse to consider other relevant factors that can make faith work, i.e. 'works'.

The same Bible that stressed the importance of faith, also stresses in James 2:26 that *"...faith, if it hath not works, is dead..."* (KJV).

Now, let us analyze what this means; this verse teaches that while faith is important, it has to be combined with "works". So what is 'works'? "Works", in this context means doing every other necessary thing to alleviate your situation. As believers, we must realize that God has given us the power to do certain things. His expectation is that we walk in that delegated authority.

Psalm 115:16 (TPT) *"The heavens belong to our God; they are His alone, but He has given us the earth and put us in charge"*.

To emphasize this, let us examine Luke 8:23-27. You can take a few minutes to read that passage before you come back to this book. The story is one that most believers are familiar with. When the disciples woke Jesus up during the storm, what did He say to them?

He said "Oh ye of little faith". That is curious, don't you think so? Little Faith? These are disciples who ran to their Lord and savior for help in times of crisis, is that not what faith is? Believing in him, despite all?

What can we imply from His response? It certainly sounded like Jesus expected more from His Disciples. Perhaps to put that little faith to work and rebuke the boisterous seas themselves, or exercise their faith, recognizing that it was impossible for the boat to capsize with the Lord of all in their company.

The revelation here is that we must understand what faith truly means. Faith is not just believing in God and knowing he would solve the problem. It is acting on our belief and taking steps accordingly.

Matthew 7:7 says *"Ask and it shall be given you; seek and ye shall find; knock and it shall be opened unto you" (KJV).*

This already means that sometimes, you must do something to get God's attention. Now, can God do miracles and defy every sense of logic and reasoning? Absolutely, He can. However, it is expedient that we do the seeking, knocking and asking.

Prayer is certainly key to healing. However we must not be ignorant of other things or people God has provided for our healing such as a word of encouragement, time of counselling, shoulder to lean on, etc. He is the source of all wisdom and knowledge. So, whilst you pray, it is not out of place to benefit from the professional knowledge in the healthcare system, including those from doctors and therapists.

Of course, God can choose to heal with or without your engagement with healthcare professionals. However, it is down to His sovereignty, mercy and the depth of your personal walk with Him.

The Role of the Church

Rick Warren, a well-known pastor and the author of "The Purpose-Driven Church" says that Christians should make sure the purpose of the church is not based on their own ideas. All churches are driven by something, e.g. finance, tradition, etc. Here are other options for the purpose of churches according to *The Great Commandment or Great Commission:*

> ➤ Worship – *praising God in music and speech;*
>
> ➤ Fellowship – *association especially with people who share one's interest or concerns;*
>
> ➤ Discipleship – *process of making someone become like Christ;*
>
> ➤ Ministry – *the work or vocation of a minister of religion;*
>
> ➤ Mission – *an important assignment carried out for religious purposes.*

What is the purpose of the church regarding mental illness?

According to Rodger Bufford, "Historically the problem of the mentally ill has been largely the responsibility of the church until the 19th Century.

However, with the scientific revolution, with the rise of Freudian psychology and its fundamentally anti-Christian perspectives and with the secularization of approaches to treatment of mental disorders which coincided with these developments, the task of dealing with mental health problems became largely secular problems." He also said, "The church had virtually abandoned its responsibility in this area". https://www.researchgate.net/publication/315802051 Christian Counseling Issues and Trends

The Church has an especially important role to play in our Christian life, as it should. As a new Christian, you are usually encouraged to join a Church and be devoted, why? This is basically because Churches have a huge impact on your Christian faith and consistent fellowship with other believers would support your growth. The Bible encourages it on the grounds that it helps spur your love for God, even the more.

Hebrews 10:24-25 (NLT)- *"And let us consider how to stir up one another to love and good works, and let us not neglect our meeting together, as some people do but encourage one another, especially now that the day of His return is drawing near".*

The essence of the Church community is that we may sharpen, encourage and care for each other. This is not an exclusive preserve of the pulpit but the pews as well.

However, despite the important role of the church in a believer's life, some churches may unconsciously fall short around mental health issues and in guiding their congregation through it. The issues are not always handled with sensitivity and understanding. This may belittle the experience of the 'sufferer', undermine their recovery and perception of the church.

CHAPTER 7: STEREOTYPES AND MISCONCEPTIONS ABOUT MENTAL HEALTH AMONG CHURCH MEMBERS

Mental health and depression are not popular topics for churches. This chapter examines the stereotypes around mental health problems in the church. I am hopeful that some light will be shed on the subject to allow us rise above them.

Since 1949, the U.S.A. has observed Mental Health Awareness month. This event provides pastors with the opportunity to discuss the subject. Mentalhealth.gov listed these commonly held false ideas:

1. *Mental health does not affect me.* The truth is one in five adult Americans will have a mental health issue.

2. *Children do not have mental health disorders.* Most children are clinically diagnosed. They can shows signs as early as 14 years of age or less.

3. *People with mental health disorders are violent.* The majority of people with mental health disorders are not violent. Only 3% to 5% of these people are dangerous.

4. *Christians are immune to mental illness.* Mental illness can affect anyone including pastors, associates, etc. It is much more prevalent in religious organizations than anyone wants to admit. Consider these statistics about Christians and mental health provided by Lifeway Research:
   - 23% of pastors admit they have struggled with a mental illness.
   - Almost 50% of pastors say they do not speak with their congregation about mental illness.
   - 59% of those actually suffering from mental illness do not speak with anyone in the church about it.
   - 32% of church worshippers say a close acquaintance or family member has died by suicide.

Naturally, many believers affected by a mental health diagnosis will turn to their social networks, churches and spiritual leaders for support, counsel and guidance, as they should. Sadly, even within the church, stigmatization is not a rare experience amongst those with mental illness. They may feel their emotional distress is trivialized or swept under the carpet. Other than silence, misguided mental health theories exist, leaving those suffering from mental illness feeling weak, ashamed, like a burden and even spiritually unclean.

A good number of believers suffering from mental illness feel vulnerable and alone. The understanding, support and care they hoped to see, are not forthcoming. Consider a U.S.A case study and examine these statistics:

- Approximately 1 in 25 adults in the U.S.A. (9.8 million or 4%) experience a serious mental illness each year that substantially interferes with or limits one or more major life activities.
- 18.1% of adults in the U.S.A experienced an anxiety disorder such as posttraumatic stress disorder, obsessive-compulsive disorder and specific phobias.

Nashville-based Lifeway Research partnered with Focus on the Family and the family of a man who endured schizophrenia to conduct a large study on faith and mental illness. One of the three groups researchers surveyed in the multi-part study was comprised of 1,000 senior Protestant pastors. As expected, based on the large numbers of Americans suffering from some form of mental illness, the Pastors were quite experienced with the subject matter.

The survey revealed that approximately three out of four Pastors said they knew at least one family member, friend or congregant who had been diagnosed with bipolar disorder. 74% said they knew someone diagnosed with clinical depression. 57% said they knew at least three people who fell into the clinical depression category.

However, the researchers found a real disconnect between the Pastors' familiarity with mental illness and how proactively their churches approached the issue. While there was a genuine desire to help those who experience mental illness, there was not a proportionate amount of concrete, supportive action. The survey showed that sometimes, while leaders are amazing at sermons and blessing their congregation, some may not be equipped enough to recognize mental health illnesses and so they may find it harder to address it. Also, while some churches are beginning to have plans to assist families affected by mental illness, there is still much work to be done.

Thankfully, more churches are beginning to be staffed with a counsellor skilled in mental illness and hopefully, soon, mental illnesses would stop being a taboo topic.

Although each Christian dealing with depression, anxiety, bipolar disorder or PTSD has a unique and personal reason for not seeking support from others not necessarily in church— there are some common experiences and misconceptions. They often get in the way of seeking life-changing help.

Here are some common stereotypes around mental health in some churches that could absolutely be corrected:

1. **TAGGING MENTAL HEALTH REALTED ISSUES AS 'SPIRITUAL'**

At times, the response to mental illness is to attribute it to a spiritual attacks. The solution therefore only resides in praying them away. This is not to disparage prayer or the place of spiritual deliverance both of which are genuine and part of the Christian faith. However, in a significant proportion of cases, spiritual oppression does not necessarily apply and mental illnesses may not always be spiritually triggered.

It is key to recognize that depression, anxiety, addiction, psychosis and other mental health issues have clearly biological and physical basis. Everyone reacts differently to challenges and issues of life. This perhaps explains why one person can shed tears when they lose a loved one and another, shows no emotions throughout the funeral. In the end, both are grieving and expressing their pain in different ways.

It should be understood that mental illness is like any other physical ailment. No one would tell a cancer or diabetic patient to simply pray about it and not seek medical help. That would be seen as irresponsible, therefore, the same proactive attitude should apply to mental illness.

My passion is to take mental health issues out of the shadows and into the mainstream discuss within the church, highlighting the need for Professional help while the church provides the much needed spiritual and social support.

However, this is not to say that mental illness cannot be a spiritual attack, it can be. In the Bible, the book of Mark Chapter 5 tells a whole story of how Jesus Christ healed a mentally disturbed man. It was documented that he was possessed by demons. From this scripture, it is not inconceivable that mental illness can be from a spiritual attack.

Some may argue that a balanced approach that tackles the root of the believer's mind-set and signposts to expert help from mental health professionals is key. Quite often, a listening ear and an understanding heart are important ingredients in the elixir that nurses them back to good mental health.

2. AVOIDING THE INDIVUDUAL WITH MENTAL HEALTH RELATED PROBLEMS

Let us face it, dealing with an individual with mental health problems is not the most pleasant experience. The doom and gloom of depression; the tears and the deafening silence or monosyllabic responses when you try to chat them up. It can be burdensome. However, rather than cast the person aside, it is the role of the church to draw near and be present. Show them the love, compassion and empathy that Jesus embodies.

It is not uncommon that people suffering from mental health problems feel the need to hide their condition, even in churches where they would otherwise feel free and comfortable. It is a wakeup call to the church. People with mental illness already face stigma and exclusion elsewhere. When they choose to turn to the church, we should be a refuge, an anchor that loves unconditionally as Jesus did.

This is the charge, we as believers have towards one another, regarding sickness and the church, Jesus Christ says it all in James 5:14 (NKJV) *"Is anyone among you sick?, Let him call for the Elders of the church and let them pray over him..."*

3. **SEEING MENTAL ILNESS AS A SIGN OF WEAKNESS:**

"Lighten up, be strong". These are examples of statements the believer dealing with mental health related issues commonly hears. While well-meaning, such statements are not always well received or helpful. We need to be sensitive to the situation and show more empathy to our brethren who have a mental health challenge.

Left with the impression that they are viewed as weak, it invalidates their feelings which are genuine. When this happens, they feel like a glitch in the body of Christ, like something is wrong with them and they have to be fixed because they are a problem.

The truth is that mental Illness or admitting same, is not a sign of weakness. They are just a natural expression of pain, trauma and sad events life throws at us. Addressing it as a glitch in the system may not solve but compound the problem.

4: BELIEVING THAT YOUR MENTAL ILLNESS IS ALWAYS BECAUSE OF YOUR SINS

This is not a pleasant or encouraging thing to hear from others as one dealing with a mental health diagnosis. It could reinforce the feeling of guilt, despair, worthlessness and hopelessness. This inaccurate image of God as the punisher and executioner, rather than the friendly and loving father brings no succor or light at the end of a deep dark tunnel.

Singer-songwriter Jennifer Knapp shared her story of lifelong management of depression - "I have experienced the best and the worst of faith-based responses to my mental health. At its worst, I have experienced utter rejection from the church. Other times, I have been counselled to absorb my sufferings as a punishment for my sins and a call to repentance".

As a church, we are the body of Christ and as such, we are called to represent His image and do what He would do. Therefore, we must remember that God loves us all, even the unbelievers and it is not in our place to judge the sinners because God loves them too.

Finally, it is noteworthy that anyone who shares our common basic humanity can be affected by mental health illness, sinner or saint. Despite his walk with God, Prophet Elijah, was depressed and suicidal at some point in his human experience. He once prayed that God should take his life and end it all. As Christian, we must recognize that all we enjoy including our health, is by God's grace and mercy, it has little to do with our status.

So, when someone around you is living with depression, anxiety, or addiction, we as the Christian community must recognize it for what it is. Our words, actions and inactions though well-meaning may be unhelpful. Let us empathize, support and show the love of Jesus.

Impact of Stigmatization of mental health

General attitudes about mental health have improved in recent years. With the disorder becoming more common, the average person knows someone who suffers from the disease. An article, "Mental Health Signs: The Impact of Age and Gender on Attitudes, published by Community Mental Health Journal, said, "Results indicate that both age and gender influence attitudes towards generalized anxiety disorders but not towards schizophrenia." These results indicate that further work needs to be done surrounding mental health.

Stigmatization in its very nature is basically when someone or a group of people see or view you in a negative light and discrimination is when they act on these views. Sadly, people struggling with mental illness in the church grapple with both stigmatization and discrimination. The ill effects are real and discussed in the following paragraphs:

1. Feelings of shame, isolation and hopelessness.

Stigma of any sort is unwarranted and for those experiencing mental illnesses, it is like kicking a person when they are down. We cover them with a cloak of shame and nudge them away from their identity in Christ.

Matthew 5:14-15 (NKJV) – *"You are the light of the world. A city that is set on a hill cannot be hidden. Nor do they light a lamp and put it under the basket, but, on a lampstand and it gives light to all who are in the house"*

When we stigmatize those with mental illness in the church, we rob of them of the privilege of being the light of the world. Someone who feels ashamed, isolates themselves and inadvertently exacerbates their underlying mental health diagnosis.

2. Reluctance to Seek Help.

No one wishes to be labelled defective, weak or lacking in faith. To avoid the stigma related to mental illness, sufferers are reluctant to open-up and seek the help they desperately need. When the church creates a safe space to be heard and provides the relevant support networks, we can begin to address this need.

3. Self-Doubt

Negative stereotypes reinforce some of the adverse symptoms of mental illness such as depression. Loss of confidence, degrading ones value and self-worth are among some of these. This naturally spirals into self-doubt and feeling of worthlessness that leads to ideas of suicide.

4. Inability to Interact.

As part of the Christian community, we should aim to interact regularly with one another. To care and check up on each other. The inherent social stigma of mental illness drives people to isolation and loneliness.

5. Guilt

The burden of guilt in the mind of someone with mental illness is made even heavier by the weight of stigma. They can be made to feel like they are to blame. Is it my sin? My ancestry or heritage?

If only I prayed and fasted hard enough or gave more, perhaps this would not have happened.

It is clear from the foregoing that stigmatization of mental illness serves no purpose other than to perpetuate the distress and suffering of the mentally unwell. It shuts people up from speaking out and/or seeking help and jeopardizes any chance of recovery. As the body of Christ, it is our calling to care and support the needy within our society, including of those with mental health challenges.

How to Counter Stereotypes surrounding Mental Illness in the Church

We have examined the various stereotypes around mental illness, its effects, and the potential impact on the Christian. Here, are some suggestions on how to counter negative stereotypes about mental illness.

To live above any form of negative stereotyping in all aspects of life, a Christian must have knowledge. Knowledge of who God is, what His word says and of who you are in Him. The bible says in *Hosea 4:6 (ESV)* *"My people are destroyed for lack of knowledge"*. Recognizing that God is great is brilliant, but more crucially knowing that He is fundamentally a good God is key to enjoying an anxiety-free life.

Jeremiah 29:11 (GWT) - *"I know the plans that I have for you, declares the Lord. They are plans for peace and not disaster, plans to give you a future filled with hope"*.

The bible is God's word and will for you. It has been tested over the ages and is infallible. Jesus overcame by the same word when He was tempted. God's word is still potent and you can counter any narrative that is contrary to what is written about you in His word.

We all need to be reminded now and again of who we are in Christ. We are the apple of His eyes, beautifully and wonderfully made. We are seated with Christ in heavenly places, far above all principalities and powers. Therefore, regardless of the challenge, look up, not down. Be rest assured that you will overcome by His grace.

Here are some ways you can deal with stigma:

1. Seek professional help:

According to a United Kingdom (UK) based survey, 35% of participants experiencing mental and emotional difficulties, did not seek any formal or informal help. Perceived stigma, difficulty expressing concerns and preference to self-reliance where barriers to accessing care. It is important to seek professional help as soon as possible to avoid the downward spiral of symptoms and potential for complication.

Mental health professionals are highly trained experts in their field. They are licensed and have regulatory bodies overseeing their practice. In the UK, your first port of call would usually be your GP. During your consultation, the GP would listen to your experiences and conduct a clinical assessment. You will both reach a shared management plan and agree on follow-up. A majority of common mental illnesses are managed in the community and you may be referred for counselling, talking therapies or started on medication. More complex conditions are referred to the Psychiatrist.

2. Do not believe it.

Another way to counter these stereotypes is not to believe them! You are not a failure, you are not possessed. It is not a weakness, neither is it the wrath of God against you. The challenges you are going through are simply normal and solutions abound. The misconceptions around mental health are so loud and when heard often enough, they are convincing. You must decide within your heart that the only thing you would believe about yourself, your feelings and your life is the word of God. Please do not be fooled by the ignorance out there into thinking less of yourself. Consider 1 Peter 2:9 (NIV) which says *"But you are a chosen people, a royal priesthood, a holy nation, God's special possession, that you may declare the praises of him who called you out of darkness into his wonderful light"*.

3. Avoid Isolation

It is often difficult to interact with others in the face of mental health stigma or discrimination. The natural tendency is to withdraw. I would recommend resisting the urge but it is easier said than done. Relate with people within your trusted support network. You could also join a mental health support group where you would meet people with similar problems and glean from their experiences and coping mechanisms. Remember, social isolation would exacerbate the symptoms.

4. Choose what defines you

Choose that you will not be defined by your illness or situation. As a believer, you should only be defined by God's word. For example, instead of saying "I'm a schizophrenic", say "I am recovering from schizophrenia". There is power in language. Consider this saying from Charles Capps - *"Jesus said, I have told my people they can have what they say but my people are saying what they have"*.

6. Do not feel attacked

Remember that people's judgement often come from a lack of understanding rather than anything else. These judgments may be preconceived based on ingrained cultural beliefs, personal experiences and biases, so do not take offense at their views, they may not know better. As believers, whether we are affected by mental health issues or we know someone dealing with it, we must recognize our responsibility to foster a supportive community – one that is inclusive, rejects discrimination and supports recovery. Here are some proven ways to help:

a) An active effort to learn more about one's mental health is a start. Congratulations, you are doing that already by reading this book. Learn the facts about mental illness and share with family, friends and colleagues.

b) Commit to understand and support people experiencing mental health challenges. In the end you will appreciate their personality rather than their illness.

c) Do not judge, label or discriminate when you meet people with mental illness. Treat all people with respect and dignity.

d) Avoid using language that puts the illness first and the person second. You could say 'a person with bipolar disorder' rather than 'that person is bipolar'.

e) Sharing your own experience of mental illness (if you have experienced it). This will help dispel myths and encourages others to do the same. Mental illness is not a sign of weakness, no one is immune.

Consider these two servants of God in the Bible:

ELIJAH AND QUEEN JEZEBEL (1 Kings 19:4)

1 Kings 19:4 (KJV) – But he himself went a day's journey into the wilderness and came and sat down under a juniper tree and he requested for himself that he might die; and said, "It is enough; now, O LORD, take away my life, for I am not better than my fathers."

Elijah did as he was told, dispatched the false prophets and demonstrated God's power. Still, he was depressed. Now he was sitting under a tree and wanted to die. God sent him an angel to comfort and feed him. *1 Kings 19:5 (NIV) - All at once, an angel touched him and said, "Get up and eat."* Hot, fresh bread and water were provided. Later an angel led him to a cave where he slept. As more trials occurred, God helped him with different provisions for different phases of the journey.

KING SAUL AND AN EVIL SPIRIT (1 SAMUEL 16:14)

Imagine life without God's love, grace and divine protection. That is what happened to King Saul when he repeatedly disobeyed God. When he failed to demonstrate the character of an Israelite king, God replaced Saul with David. Saul became fretful, suspicious, anxious and distracted. He was dethroned and lost his royal house. *1 Samuel 16:14 (KJV) "But the spirit of the LORD departed from Saul and an evil spirit from the Lord troubled him".*

With all these being said, the importance of God's word cannot be overemphasized. His thoughts towards you are thoughts of good and it is important that you are reminded of that every day. So, whenever the devil whispers accusation and guilt, or you are stressed, revert to this section for a refresher.

Speaking of the mind, as far as it relates to mental health, we are admonished to have the mind of Christ. What does the mind of Christ mean as it relates to the believer's mental health? This will be explored in the next chapter.

CHAPTER 8:
UNDERSTANDING THE MIND OF CHRIST IN RELATION TO MENTAL HEALTH

What does it mean to have the mind of Christ, yet grapple with MENTAL health diagnosis like anxiety and depression?

As we navigate those emotionally exhausting dark days, the mind of Christ is all about reorienting our mindset: Who are we in Christ, really? Here are seven crucial points to consider and help you find an encouraging Biblical viewpoint on depression, anxiety and other mental health challenges.

The Biblical Perspective

1. **The mind of Christ is God's true perspective about you.**
   "Now, we have not received the spirit of the world, but rather the Spirit who is from God, that we might know the things freely given to us by God." - 1

Corinthians 2:12 (KJV). Mental health challenges can distort our emotions and thoughts, making it difficult to thrive spiritually, grow in faith and trust God completely. It can feel like keeping faith takes all the energy you can muster and you lack enough emotional or physical stamina to "push through". Having the mentality of Christ, on the other hand, is more about resting in our truest identity in Christ and recognizing what we have freely received from Him. It is this that moulds and empowers us to face another day.

2. **The mind of Christ speaks to His love and Spirit at rest within us.** God's love gives us the full assurance that we are His children. John 1:12-13 (NKJV) says *"But as many as received Him, to them He gave the right to become children of God, to those who believe in His name: who were born, not of blood, nor of the will of the flesh, nor of the will of man, but of God".*

Therefore, you can be rest assured that even when mental health stressors muddle up your faith and you strive to believe in Him, He believes in you because you are important to Him (Isaiah 43:4 (ESV) *"....precious in my eyes..."*). Jeremiah 31:3 (ESV) also says, *"I have loved you with an everlasting love; therefore, I have continued my faithfulness to you".*

So, sadness and anxiety or any other condition, cannot change the depth and breadth of His everlasting love towards us. Also Romans 8:38 (NLT) *says "And I am convinced that nothing can ever separate us from God's love. Neither death nor life, neither angels nor demons, neither our fears for today nor our worries about tomorrow—not even the powers of hell can separate us from God's love".* Regardless of our failings and inadequacies, Jesus draws us closer to gently remind us of His love!

3. **The mind of Christ reassures you of His constant presence.** *"....Can a woman forget her nursing child, And not have compassion on the son of her womb? Surely they may forget, yet I will not forget you. See, I have inscribed you on the palms of My hands; Your walls are continually before Me", Isaiah 49:15-16 (NKJV).* When dealing with mental health issues we frequently feel detached or distant from God. It is most likely the symptoms of mental illness, not necessarily

a separation from God that is responsible for the feeling of disconnect.

Having the mind of Christ means having a permanent connection to the presence of Jesus and all His blessings for every aspect of our lives. According to scriptures, we are *"seated with Christ in Heavenly places"* Ephesians 2:6 (NKJV). This means that we are placed in the same victorious life, lacking nothing from it and always having His unending grace and mercy for all our challenges (see Hebrews 4:16).

4. **The Mind of Christ teaches reliance on God, our endless source.** Regardless of how we feel the God is near. His presence is always accompanied by fullness of joy and His desire to bless us. Psalm 23:1-2 (NJKV) says, *"The LORD is my shepherd, I shall not want, He makes me to lie down in green pastures; He leads me beside the still waters"*. As our good shepherd, it means we will never lack anything. Jesus is continually leading us to safety, rest and plenty of food and water, all the while being protected by a loving Shepherd. Our Shepherd heals, fills and restores our souls - because that is what His name and character are all about (Psalm 23:3).

Now, you may be asking yourself questions like: What if I am alone? What if no one understands? What if it is painfully lonely? May I ask you to try one thing? Look to the heavens, let this feeling of loneliness turn into a solitude experience where you can lean on and learn from the Shepherd. God's face and hands are not distant from our isolation or feeling of it. He knows exactly just how you feel, He understands and can restore you. Hebrew 4:15 (NKJV) *"for we do not have a High Priest who cannot sympathize with our weaknesses but was in all point tested as we are but without sin"*.

So, pray, "Father, help me, give me strength through this!" Personally, I have been there too, and He saw me through that patch. Ultimately, Jesus said the Holy Spirit, the Comforter, would abide and guide us (John 14:16 and 26).

5. **The mind of Christ focuses on new life, not on your sins or failures.** With sadness and anxiety, there is a lot of self-criticism and a constant attempt to disqualify yourself from grace. This often leads to a lot of self-blame, judgment and attempts to get back into God's good graces by our strength. "The mind of Christ is not for

a willpower sin-management or keeping religious disciplines in fear". To begin with, "God does not view us through a sin-filter or treat us in light of our sin-failure" (see Psalm 103:10). God views us through the lens of His love and compassion, always! Jesus demonstrates what the Father is like with His broken-hearted son, just as He did in the narrative of the prodigal son. *"And he arose and came to his father. But while he was still a long way off, his father saw him and felt compassion and ran and embraced him and kissed him"* Luke 15:20 (KJV).

Regardless of how unworthy, depressed, anxious or distant from Him you may feel, God is reaching out to you with love and compassion, eager to embrace and restore.

Furthermore, we are in Christ, called to enjoy all of God's riches at Christ's expense. We are partakers of His divine nature and have all His love and blessings at our disposal (Ephesians 1:3).

Do not let anyone tell you any differently, as a Christian, you are complete in Him. Colossians 2:8-10 (NKJV) tells us, *"Beware lest anyone cheat you through philosophy and empty deceit, according to the tradition of men, according to the basic principles of the world, and not according to Christ. For in Him dwells all the fullness of the Godhead bodily; and you are complete in Him, who is the head of all principality and power."*

Be mindful and live consciously of who you are and whose you are. Intimately know how right we are (righteousness, justification) in Christ and the abundant comfort and grace we have been endowed with (2 Corinthians 5:21).

"This is what it means to have the mind-set of Christ. The mind of Christ guides you through any mental health stressor to help renew your mind (perspective), reconstruct your heart (resilience) and realign your life (with creative strengths) for greater and healthier outcomes".

6. **The mind of Christ always reminds you that you are worthy, a constant value without performance.** A writer once said "The mind of Christ means God's mind about you is already made up, and His thoughts concerning you are always good and pleasing". How true, Jeremiah 29:11 (NKJV) says. *"For I know the thoughts that I*

think toward you, says the LORD, thoughts of peace and not of evil, to give you a future and a hope".

In God's sight and on the strength of the finished work on Calvary (Jesus's death and resurrection) you are redeemed and innocent. He affirms His love for you and rejoices in the fact that you are His! Psalm 139:17(NLT) says, *"How precious are your thoughts about me, O God. They cannot be numbered".*

Mental health pressures can make you oblivious of these truths and even antagonistic toward God. However, Jesus knows and desires to show you His delight in you (Psalm 18:19 and Psalm 149:4). God's restoration is about being His delight, *"You shall no more be termed Forsaken ... Desolate, but you shall be called, My Delight is in her..." (Isaiah 62:4-ESV).* This is the Jesus in your depression or anxiety diagnosis. Though mental health challenges make our minds race in negative spirals, even disgust, God's mind is already made up about us and He says, "We are good, you are good and I will be with you".

7. **Your mind of Christ reframes your identity into beauty and gives you strength to walk.**

Here is a fallacy that often accompanies our mental health challenges. Whether it is the doom and gloom of depression, the intrusive thoughts to end it all or the deep anxiety about tomorrow, there is a risk that we see ourselves through the prism of a "FALSE sin bias". The misconception that we are broken beyond repair, sinners beyond redemption, a failure of the faith and vulnerable to the enemy's onslaught. That God is somehow allowing all this to punish us. This sadly perpetuates the so called "Learned Helplessness", the tendency to remain in the abyss, too weak to try, making it hard to move forward.

There is hope, God has made a way. Step into it, hold on to Him. Ask Him for light and help in this dark tunnel. His word in Isaiah 62:3-4 (NKJV) redefines you:

[3] *"You shall be a crown of beauty in the hand of the Lord, a royal diadem in the hand of your God" (an intimate part of His royal love, you are adorning beauty to Him).* [4] *"You shall no longer be called Forsaken, and you shall no longer be called Desolate, but you shall be called, My Delight is in her".*

I hear you; it might feel hard to counter the false narrative on dark days, when you feel more broken than delightful. Look up, there is a God that loves you more than life itself, just because you are worth it (see John 3:16). He is your advocate, a friend that sticks closer than a brother and a present help in this time of need. Lean on Him.

How to renew your mind.

The Lord is needed to renew the Mind (Romans 12:2)

As a person dealing with a mental illness, you may wish you could push a reset button and have your mind renewed. Well, in a way, you can. When you pray and ask God for help, He intervenes as only He can. *Romans 12:2(KJV) says "And be not conformed to this world: but be ye transformed by the renewing of your mind, that you prove what is that good, and acceptable, and perfect, will of God".*

Spirit of Power

The Bible tells us in *2 Timothy 1:7 (NKJV) says "For God has not given us a spirit of fear, but of power..."* He empowers us to be made strong in our weakness. Whenever you do not know what to do, call on Jesus!

Luke 10:17 (KJV) – *"And the seventy returned again with joy, saying, Lord even the devils are subject unto us through thy name"*.

Meditation: This means to mutter, ponder, speak quietly or read a verse of scripture over and over again. It requires you to think deeply of God's word, allowing the Holy Spirit to reveal the truth or message behind the letters. *"…for the letter kills but the Spirit gives life"* (2 Corinthians 3:6b, ESV).

Consider Joshua 1:8 (NKJV), which says *"This Book of the Law shall not depart from your mouth, but you[a] shall meditate in it day and night, that you may observe to do according to all that is written in it. For then you will make your way prosperous, and then you will have good success"*.

Rest in God

Resting in God means trusting in Him. There are more than thirty scriptures that mention rest. Matthew 11:28 (KJV) says *"Come unto me, all ye that labor and are heavy laden, and I will give you rest"*.

Promise of Peace

John 14:27 (NKJV) says "Peace I leave with you. My peace I give to you, not as the world gives do I give to you; Let not your heart be troubled, neither it be afraid". You have already been given peace. So when it seems like you do not have it, just dig deeper. Access what was freely given.

Cast Your Fears

In 1 Peter 5:7 (NKJV), God says *"Casting all your care upon Him for He cares for you."* Did you notice the term *cast*? It does not say rest, leave or give your fears. It says *cast* or throw. It is a vigorous effort that is done with energy and deliberateness as well as confidence. The second part tells us why - because He cares for us. We can be assured that God will handle it, not because He is Almighty and all-knowing but because He loves us.

CHAPTER 9:
MENTAL ILLNESS AND AVAILABLE TREATMENTS

As with physical illness, thankfully, there are treatment options for the management of mental health disorders. There are a wide range of them and based on best available evidence. Treatment ranges from talking therapies to self-care measure and medication. There is no reason not to explore these options with your mental health professionals whilst in praying and trusting God for wholeness.

Pharmacological and non-pharmacological treatments

Prescriptions and Side Effects

As a Christian with a mental health disorder, your GP or Psychiatrist may recommend drug therapy and decide which medication is right for you. Broadly speaking and depending on the underlying diagnosis, your doctor may prescribe anti-depressants, mood stabilizers, anti-anxiety medication or antipsychotics.

Please note that the benefits of some of these drugs are not usually felt immediately until at least two to three weeks of treatment. Sometimes your symptoms may even appear worse initially, but you are encouraged to continue. However, if you are experiencing unwanted or serious side effect, kindly contact your doctor as there may well be an alternative medication. Once established on treatment, it is advisable that you do not stop the medication abruptly. This may result in serious withdrawal adverse effects or worsening of symptoms.

Every drug we take can have side effects, so your prayer should be that you would experience the benefits rather the unwanted side effects. Whichever medication you decide to try, please ensure it is done with prayer. *"He heals the brokenhearted and binds up their wounds" Psalm 147:3 (NKJV)*

Non-pharmacological Interventions for Mental Disorders					
S/N	Treatment	Disorder	Benefits	Side Effects

1.	Talk Therapy	Depression, anxiety, mood disorder	Personal changes	--
2.	Counseling	Depression, anxiety, mood disorder	Communication, behavior	--
3.	Cognitive Behavioral Therapy (CBT)	Depression, anxiety, mood disorder	Rational thoughts	--
4.	Self Care	Depression, anxiety, mood disorder	Stress Management, Health	--
5.	Interpersonal	Depression, anxiety,	Improved Relationships	--

	Therapy (IPT)	mood disorder		

Talk Therapy

Talk therapy is the treatment of mental, emotional and behavioral disorders requiring dialogue listening and advice from a certified mental health professional.

Counseling

This refers to the provision of help and guidance in managing personal, professional, social or psychological problems by a certified professional.

Cognitive Behavioral Therapy

A type of therapy that includes negative thought patterns about the self and the world are questioned in order to challenge reality and unwanted behaviors.

Self- care

This is the practice of taking action to improve one's health.

Interpersonal Therapy

This is a time-limited, focused, evidenced-based method used to treat mood disorders.

Herbs, Tinctures, Teas, and Exercise

Of course, God has provided natural remedies for whatever ails us. *Ezekiel 47:12 (ESV) says "And on the banks, on both sides of the river, there will grow all kinds of trees for food...Their fruit will be for food, and their leaves for healing"*.

Chamomile, valerian root and skullcap promote calmness. Since Hippocrates' time, kava kava, St. John's work and lemon balm have been used to treat anxiety. Massages and reflexology can stimulate receptors under the skin and can lower blood pressure and cortisol levels. Also, a pet can provide excellent companionship.

Food affects how you feel. Reduce intake of sugar, sugar substitutes and processed foods. Choose all-natural foods like fruits, vegetables, rice, beans and wheat bread. Keep a food diary and note the effects of food regarding your mind and body.

Aerobic exercises, including jogging, swimming, cycling, gardening and even dancing can reduce anxiety and depression by increasing blood circulation to the brain. It also influences the hypothalamic-pituitary-adrenal and mediates the body's reaction to stress. A strong, healthy body is beneficial. *Proverbs 24:5 (ESV) says "A wise man is full of strength, and a man of knowledge enhances his might..."*

Christians and Yoga

Yoga does not fit with Christianity. It would be difficult to do the stretches without the meditation aspect. According to Kitchen Stewardship, a Christian-based teaching, Christians practicing yoga are similar to an atheist taking the Eucharist. He could say that he does not believe that it is the body of Christ. However, that does not mean it is not true. There are numerous exercise programs you could try. Yoga is a Hindu spiritual exercise. Sometimes demonic spirits come in because we unwittingly opened the door.

The Problem with Hypnosis

As a Christian, you should not be concerned about anything that does not match biblical teachings. Hypnosis involves someone else controlling your mind while you are unconscious or fully awake. *Matthew 7:15 (ESV) says "Beware of false prophets, which come to you in sheep's clothing, but inwardly they are ravening wolves".*

Addressing Issues about Mental Health

Communicating about mental health is not easy, however it does not have to be difficult. Follow these suggestions:

- ➢ Schedule a time that is convenient without any distractions.
- ➢ Let the person with the illness talk as much or as little as they would like.
- ➢ Do not play doctor and try and diagnose their illness.
- ➢ Ask open-ended questions that will not hinder the conversation.
- ➢ Listen carefully to what is being said and consider repeating it back to them to make certain you heard it correctly.

CHAPTER 10: THE MENTAL HEALTH RESOURCES AVAILABLE TO CHRISTIANS

This chapter focuses on materials that are available to Christians regarding their mental health. These materials and groups do not necessarily make you a mental health professional or expert, but they are better than doing nothing. They would make you more knowledgeable about these issues and put you on the path to recovery.

Mental Health Charities

Mental Health Grace Alliance: This organization is a Christ-centered, multi-faceted resource for people with mental illnesses and their families. The emphasis is on healing and coping with a mental health problem. They offer support groups for persons with mental illnesses and their families, as well as counselling and leadership training for those seeking to recover from a mental health crisis.

Fresh Hope: Pastor Brad Hoefs, who suffers from bipolar disorder, started this organization. He is aware of the difficulties of ministering and living with a major mental illness. This is a Christ-centred support organization that trains churches to form peer support groups for people with mental illnesses and their loved ones.

Hope for Mental Health Starter Kit: This resource from Saddleback Church provides a variety of multimedia assets that congregations of all sizes can utilize to start their own mental health ministry.

National Alliance on Mental Illness (NAMI): NAMI describes itself as "America's largest grassroots mental health organization dedicated to improving the lives of individuals and families affected by mental illness." The organization provides information, advocacy, support groups, referrals and more. NAMI exists in part to give the kind of support some churches and their leaders require, despite the fact that it is not a faith-based organization.

Mental Health First Aid: This training prepares people to respond effectively to mental health crises as first responders. Why not have at least one trained member of staff in your congregation?

Pathways to Promise: A resource for people of all faiths that seeks to "enable the religion community's efforts in reaching out to those with mental illnesses and their families". They provide congregations and their leaders with information and resources, some of which are tailored specifically to Christian ministry.

Friends from various Christian charities and church leadership roles have been talking about how the local church can be resourced in mental and emotional health. Every church could establish a network of local psychiatrists, psychologists, therapists, and social workers who specialize in a variety of areas. Refer individuals to them if they need professional mental health care or emotional support and consider using them as a resource for yourself and your employees.

The resources and support listed below are available to you. Here are a couple of other materials and sites that Christians can find help regarding mental illnesses.

Kintsugi Hope: Kintsugi Hope, a charity set up by Patrick and Diane Regan in 2017, exists to make a positive difference to people's emotional and mental Wellbeing. Kintsugi Hope regularly holds or takes part in speaking events, raising awareness on mental health and stigma as well as acting as a driving force to open up conversations on topics many find difficult.

Mind and Soul Foundation

(www.mindandsoulfoundation.org): This is a national charity that seeks

- To Educate: Sharing the best of Christian theology and scientific Advances.
- To Equip: Helping people meet with God and recover from Emotional distress.
- To Encourage: Engaging with the local church and Mental health services.

Renew Wellbeing

(www.renewwellbeing.org.uk): A national charity for training and supporting churches to open simple safe Sustainable places where 'it is ok not to be ok.'

"Read Slow Down, Show up and Pray" by Ruth Rice, published by Authentic Media (2021) tells the story of how Renew Wellbeing and provides Practical advice for setting up a Renew Wellbeing centre in your church and locality.

Sanctuary (www.sanctuarymentalhealth.org/uk):

The Sanctuary Course from Sanctuary UK is a free online resource to grow mental health Awareness, offering a space to share experiences and tackle stigma. Combining elements of psychology, theology and lived experience Sanctuary UK offers a range of resources and training to support a wholesome church approach to mental health and wellbeing.

TalkThrough (www.talkthrough.org.uk):

TalkThrough offers a combination of resources that aim to equip youth workers, parents, churches and schools to attend to wellbeing issues. Renew Wellbeing is working with TalkThrough to develop training for youth and families, Renew Children, Youth and Families (Renew CYF).

Church of England Resources

- **Supporting Good Mental Health by Professor Chris Cook:** This is available as a booklet (pdf format) and 13 audio reflections aimed at supporting mental health.
- **BAME Mental Health Tool-Kit**: This is provided by the Church of England's Mission and Public Affairs Department Resources for those in Ministry.

- **I want a Christian Psychiatrist by David Enoch (Monarch Books, 2006):** This is a very helpful Book by a Christian psychiatrist about mental illness and how/why Christians should accept psychiatric help.

Other Agencies and Resources

- **Mental Health Foundation**

(https://www.mentalhealth.org.uk/):

This foundation works to prevent mental health problems by community programs, Research, public engagement and advocacy. This website has a wealth of useful and reliable information.

- **Mind** (www.mind.org.uk): This is a National Charity offering comprehensive information on all aspects of mental Health.

- **Royal College of Psychiatrists**

(https://www.rcpsych.ac.uk/mental-health):

The professional body responsible for training and standards in psychiatry. The Mental health information section of their website offers useful resources for patients and care givers.

- **COVID-19: Psychological First Aid**

(https://www.futurelearn.com/courses/psychological-first-aid-covid-19): This provides training to help people cope with the mental distress due to COVID-19

- **Mental Health First Aid Training**

(https://mhfaengland.org/): This provides workplace based training to support good mental health.

- **NHS**: the NHS provides a list of mental health charity helplines, access to local NHS Emergency helplines and online CBT that is accessible via referral by your GP. https://www.nhs.uk/mental-health/nhs-voluntary-charity-services/charity-andvoluntary-services/get-help-from-mental-health-helplines/

National Institute of Mental Health: The website of this federal government agency is packed with information about mental health and specific mental diseases, as well as access to additional resources.

Mental Health Apps: The solution to feeling better may just be a click away. Mental health apps like Moodfit, Talkspace, Sanvello are available on GooglePlay. They have features like access to professional help and assistance with self-diagnosis. Be sure to also check out Christian apps like Bible Gateway, She Reads Truth and Prayer Mate.

Resources For young people

In Grampian (Scotland), young people are generally referred to CAMHS (Child and Adolescent Mental Health Services). Here is a Comprehensive list of organizations providing help for young people

- https://www.talkthrough.org.uk/resources
- www.beheadstrong.uk – this is run by Youths cape the Christian youth charity offering resources and information from a faith- informed perspective
- www.youngminds.org.uk – This organization offer resources and opportunities for young people to share their experiences of mental health, as well as the services of qualified therapists and counsellors for ongoing support
- https://www.bacp.co.uk/about-therapy/we-can-help/ - this is the National accredited body of counsellors and psychotherapists.
- https://www.psychotherapy.org.uk/ - This is the UK body for registered psychotherapists
- https://www.acc-uk.org/ - This is the Association of Christian Counsel

CHAPTER 11: THE POWER OF HABITS

A healthy mind is just as important as a healthy body. As the saying goes, "there is no health without mental health". However, we often overlook the importance of developing habits that foster self-confidence, emotional stability and security. It is common knowledge that healthy nutrition and exercise builds our physical health, but what steps can we take to ensure that we are emotionally resilient? Here are a few suggestions complied by experts in the field of mental health:

1. PRIOTIZE REST:

We spend around a third of our lives in bed and sleep is just as vital as eating, drinking and breathing. Going just a couple of days without a good night's sleep can have a huge impact on our emotions, memory and critical thinking abilities.

A common misunderstanding about people with mental health concerns is that they could just 'pull themselves together' or 'get up and do something!', but in reality, it is probably more important that these issues are understood and addressed, as they can often both be contributing factors and side effects of mental illness.

Ensure regular sleep schedule and stick to it. Go to bed at a set time and this means no television or mobile phones! In fact, it is probably best to keep screens out of the room altogether if possible. You should only go to bed when you intend to sleep.

The brain is fantastic at making connections. It is important that it connects the bedroom with the act of sleep. Ensure the bedroom is dark, comfortable and free from distractions. If you cannot sleep, consider some quiet music or reading a book for a while and you will hopefully find yourself nodding off to sleep. This is called **Sleep hygiene.**

2. MAKE EFFORTS TO THINK POSITIVELY

In the face of depression, positivity can feel like a herculean task - easier said than done. Consciously develop an optimistic attitude to life and focus on the good in any given situation. It is not turning a blind eye to harsh realities, it is a mind-set of approaching situations with an outlook that it will all end in praise.

This is indeed true for us as Christians. Romans 8:28 (NKJV) says *"And we know that all things work together for good to those who love God, to those who are called according to His purpose"*. A working understanding of this scripture allows us as Christians believe the good in all circumstances.

Every morning, declare aloud, "today is going to be a good day!" There is power in declarations. Positive words reinforce a positive mindset. When something good happens, notice and acknowledge it! We are all too often distracted by the bad and the ugly, forgetting all the good in our lives. Pay special attention to the good things in your life, even if they are small. Like little drops they will eventually form a tidal wave of gratitude and showers of joy.

3. EXERCISE AND EAT WELL

It may sound cliché but the saying 'healthy body, healthy mind' is true! We are biological machines, and if we use the wrong type of fuel or allow our joints to 'rust' then everything else will be impacted.

Exercise naturally reduces anxiety, improves sleep and relieves stress. It enhances the feeling of wellbeing through the release of feel-good chemicals in the brain such as endorphins.

According to a 2019 study by Harvard T.H. Chan School of public health, running for 15 minutes a day or walking for an hour reduces the risk of major depression by 26%.

Are you thinking of exercising? The best time to start was yesterday. Consider the FITT principle *(Frequency, Intensity, Time, Type) which states that, "exercise is an activity that stimulates the body to adapt and become stronger. The stimulus has to be appropriate to derive health benefits. If the stimuli is too light the body will not adapt, if too high, it may cause injury'.* Exercise should be personalised. You should choose what works for you. Duration should be at least between 75 and 150 minutes a week .This can be either moderate intensity such as walking, hiking, riding a bike or more vigorous activities like running, swimming, skipping with a rope or aerobics. So just taking a 30-minute walk for fresh air can have a huge impact on your body.

Ensure you eat plenty vegetables, fruits, nuts, high fiber carbohydrate (to make up about one third of your food portion) and fish (including portions of oily fish).

Avoid processed or junk food and saturated fats (butter, fatty red meat), unsaturated fats are preferred (oily fish, avocado, olive oil). Cut down your intake of refined sugar, salt, alcohol and quit smoking. Drink six to eight glasses of water a day. Consider brushing up on your culinary skills to bring out the best from your ingredients without compromising on taste. You will be amazed at what difference small changes make to your mood.

4. TAKE BREAKS

We live in a high pressure, fast paced world. The presence of the internet and social media means that information is disseminated quickly. We are always on the go, absorbing information and responding emotionally. In some ways this is great, we are more connected than ever before. We can communicate with friends and family wherever they are and we have new support networks available to us that were absent twenty years ago.

However, their unbridled use can be a source of sleep deprivation, stress and anxiety. Therefore, practice some self-care. Ensure to set aside some time for yourself ("Me Time"). Go out and take in some natural scenery. Spend some time away from screens, social media and the couch assimilating negative current affairs. It is alright to have some downtime to relax, reflect, rejuvenate and re-strategize. Get yourself ready to take on tomorrow with its challenges.

5. HAVE A HOBBY

In a recent (2020) study by Fancourt et al., it was revealed that having a hobby is linked to lower levels of depression. Team based hobbies may promote interaction and avoid loneliness, giving one a sense of belonging. Physical hobbies can improve your fitness. Hobbies like playing a musical instrument can improve your memory while others like board-game puzzles and reading can limit the risk of developing dementia in later life.

6. CHANGE YOUR MINDSET

Your mind is the seat of thought, feeling and faculty of consciousness. It is crucial to our reasoning and decision making. So, it is an especially important facet of who we are. Our mind set is formed by what we read, hear and see, over time. Our mind is a battle ground, "the decisions, you make, the words you speak and the actions you take, begins in the mind" (Joyce Meyer).

Consequently, we should endeavor to think positively, think success, think greatness and eventually it becomes your reality. Kindly consider these scriptures:

Proverbs 23:7 (KJV): *"For as he thinketh in his heart, so is he".*

Philippians 4:8 (NKJV) "*Finally, brethren, whatever things are true, whatever things are noble, whatever things are lovely…."*

We are all a product of our minds and our thoughts. When your heart is right, you will think positive thoughts.

In Matthew 12:34(ESV), Jesus said…. "*Out of the abundance of the heart, the mouth speaks".*

Proverbs 4:23-27(NLT) says *"Guard your heart above all else, for it determines the course of your life".*

As a believer, your mind and heart is one of your greatest assets, so this should be guarded jealously!

7. IT IS OKAY TO BE VULNERABLE, SOMETIMES

Despite all our best efforts, it can sometimes still feel difficult to be honest about your struggles with mental health. We may not predict people's reaction, this could be daunting. Being honest with yourself, allowing yourself to be vulnerable and asking for help is an important part of staying mentally healthy. We are not invincible, everyone struggles sometimes. A chat with a trusted friend may be the first bold step to your recovery.

MAINTAINING GOOD MENTAL HEALTH

The demands of this world can affect anyone, especially a Christian struggling with mental illness. Last year when COVID-19 struck, no one was prepared for it, but we got through it one step at a time. The Bible tells us to be of good courage. *Joshua 1:9 (NKJV) says "Have I not commanded you? Be strong and of good courage; do not be afraid, nor be dismayed, for the LORD your God is with you wherever you go."*

Peace Be Still

Jesus and the apostles were in a ship out on the sea when a storm arose. Jesus was asleep and the apostles were afraid. *Mark 4:39(NKJV) says "And He arose and rebuked the wind, and said to the sea," Peace, be still!" And the wind ceased and there was a great calm".* You will have storms in your life. It is inevitable but all you have to do is call on Jesus.

God is Near to Brokenhearted

It is okay to be sad or lonely, but know that you are never alone. *Psalm 34:18 (NKJV) says "The LORD is near to those who have a broken heart; and saves such as have a contrite spirit".*

Testing of Faith and Maturity

Sometimes God allows us to undergo trials to strengthen us. *Hebrews 11:17 says "By faith Abraham, when he was tested, offered up Isaac, and he who had received the promises offered up his only begotten son, , of whom it was said, "In Isaac your seed shall be called. "* Also, *James 1:3 (ESV) says "For you know that the testing of your faith produces steadfastness."* One thing is certain, God will not give you more than you can bear. *1 Corinthians 10:13 (TPT) assures us that*

"We all experience[a] times of testing,[b] which is normal for every human being. But God will be faithful to you. He will screen and filter the severity, nature, and timing of every test or trial you face[c] so that you can bear it. And each test is an opportunity to

trust him more, for along with every trial God has provided for you a way of escape that will bring you out of it victoriously".

MANAGING THE BUSYNESS OF LIFE: DISTRACTORS THAT AFFECT YOUR MENTAL HEALTH

Busyness vs. Solitude

Are you busy as in "productive" way or are you preoccupied with doing stuff that does not really matter. In today's hectic world, people are always talking on their phone, watching television or surfing the internet. Is that how a Christian should spend their time?

In *Luke 5:16 (NKJV) says this about Jesus "and He Himself often withdrew into the wilderness and prayed"*. Do you have a time for prayer? Do you make time for private

Bible Study? Take an assessment of how you use your time.

Put God First

Matthew 6:33 (NKJV) "But seek first the kingdom of God and His righteousness, and all these things will be added to you ". In between work, school and family obligations, where does God fall in your life? Do you start your mornings off with prayer or do you leave it to be done after everything else in your life? Starting your day with the Lord can guarantee a stress-free day; this is not to say that challenges would not arise, but you would have the mental wherewithal to overcome it. This has worked for me repeatedly.

Putting God first is a literal expression. He must be a priority, not an afterthought. *"Trust in the LORD with all your heart and do not lean on your own understanding" (Proverbs 3:5-6, ESV).* Often times our anxieties stem from wrong or hasty decisions, but when they are directed by the Holy Spirit, success is certain and we will have no regrets. Prioritization is essential, it does not take much time, perhaps only thirty minutes, but it makes a whole world of difference.

Posts, Pictures and Gossip

In Philippians 4:8 (NLT) the Bible says *"And now, dear brothers and sisters, one final thing. Fix your thoughts on what is true and honorable, and right and pure and lovely and admirable. Think about things that are excellent and worthy of praise."*

Teenagers in Britain may be putting their health and education at risk by spending too much time on social media at bedtime, according to a major study into adolescent sleep habits. Researchers found out that more than a third of teenagers spent at least three hours a day on social media, with a fifth devoting at least five hours to the activity.

According to an article in the Guardian Newspaper, Adolescents in Britain may be risking bad grades and emotional issues as a result of excessive activity on social media. Apparently, posting pictures and commenting on their favorite online platforms for three or more hours is associated with insufficient sleep, obesity and a range of mental health problems. Let us spend more time on things that matter!

These are interesting times, the COVID -19 pandemic has brought to sharp focus, what is important in life. As we spent more time with our families and worried about matters of life and death, our God-given values took center stage.

For a Christian with a mental illness, spending time alone at home with limited human contact can be quite tough, but not impossible. Prayer is always available. As we rely on prayer, we realize our dependence on God – something that can be forgotten or taken for granted with the everyday hustle and bustle of life.

The most important thing to remember as a Christian facing a mental illness is that you are not helpless. You have choices. With technology, medications and alternative health treatments, you can explore new options. Furthermore, you can empower yourself by talking about it with a trusted friend. There is no reason to be ashamed. You are not alone. With your steadfast trust in God, you can be strengthened to manage your mental health. Remember there is no health without mental health.

References

Adams, A. "How Mental Health Alters Decision Making. https://news.stanford.edu/features/2015/decisions/disease-state.html. 10/16/15

American Addiction Centers. Children of Alcoholics: The Impacts of Alcoholics on Kids. https://americanaddictioncenters.org/alcoholism-treatment/children. 08/02/21

Center for Anxiety Disorders. What is Trauma? https://centerforanxietydisorders.com/what-is-trauma/

Fancourt D., Opher S., De Oliveira C. Fixed Effect Analysis of Time/Varying Associations between Hobbies and Depression in a Longitudinal Cohort Study Psychother Psychosom 2020, 89: 111-113

Fusion Church. What is Christianity? Https://fusionchurchny.com/what-is-christianity-and-how-is-it-different-from-other-world-religions/?gclid=CjwKCAjwpMOIBhBAEiwAy5M6YAjccQ8CkImW6sYNM7Y2Bpwo_Ck0dUG4RXFd-ja_0T3LniAS9mlQvRoC2gUQAvD_BwE

Hyman, S. Mental Health Depression Needs Large Human Genetics.

https://www.researchgate.net/profile/Steven-Hyman-3/publication/268234746_Mental_health_Depression_needs_large_human-genetics_studies/links/5a753fae45851541ce566c24/Mental-health-Depression-needs-large-human-genetics-studies.pdf

McManus S., Bebbington P., Jenkins R., Brugha T. Mental health and wellbeing in England: Adult Psychiatric Morbidity Survey 2014 [Internet]. Leeds; 2016. Available from: **content.digital.nhs.uk**

Mental Health Foundation

https://www.mentalhealth.org.uk/

Mental Health Taskforce NE. The Five Year Forward View for Mental Health. 2016 [cited 2017 May 23]; Available from: **england.nhs.uk**

Ritchie H., Roser M., Mental Health [Internet]. 2018 [cited 2019 Sep 6]. Available from: **ourworldindata.org**

Sadler K., Vizard T., Ford T., Goodman A., Goodman R., Mcmanus S. Mental Health of Children and

Young People in England, 2017: Trends and characteristics [Internet]. 2018 [cited 2019 Jan 7]. Available from: **digital.nhs.uk**

Salaheddin K., Mason B. (2016) Identifying barriers to mental health help-seeking among young adults in the UK: a cross-sectional survey. Br J Gen Pract doi:10.3399/bjgp16X687313

Swedish Nomad. Facts about Christianity. **https://www.swedishnomad.com/facts-about-christianity/**

University of Maine. Children and Brain Development: What We Know About How Children Learn. **Https://extension.maine.edu/publications/4356e**

J. Padilla, 4 Ways to Understand the Mind of Christ in Depression or Anxiety — Grace Alliance (mentalhealthgracealliance.org)

- The Holy Bible
- The Stigma Around Mental Illness for Christians - Geneva College, a Christian College in Pennsylvania (PA)
- https://www.archcareservices.co.uk/7-habits-that-encourage-good-mental-health/

- https://www.crcna.org/news-and-events/news/new-mental-health-resources-available-faith-leaders
- https://www.psychiatry.org/patients-families/warning-signs-of-mental-illness

Printed in Great Britain
by Amazon